Here it is: hooked-on-phonics for Christian. incredible handbook for changing the world, a sort of Revolution 101. As with most prophets, Ruth was ahead of the times (hence another 'revised' edition here). But this book is bound to be a guide for the contemporary church, which is increasingly aware that our faith in the God of heaven has to affect the way we live on Earth.
*Shane Claiborne, author, activist and recovering sinner*

Ruth has a rare ability to change a person's way of seeing the world and, at the same time, provide very practical steps for living out that new way of seeing the world. She's done that for me. Because of Ruth, I see caring for God's beautiful world as a natural part of following Christ and I have plenty of simple ways to put that faith into action. This book will do the same for you.
*Jeff Galley, Central LifeGroups and Missions Leader, Life.Church, USA*

Ruth Valerio is a true pioneer. She has made a humble and practical journey in caring for creation through years of trial and error, and her book allows us to understand the grateful relationship with God that has been the life-spring of her different and creative way of living. *L is for Lifestyle* brings us all the benefit of Ruth's hard-won experience and applied faith; it will be an essential resource for all who are concerned to live the whole of their lives to God's glory, and for the healing of his creation.
*Peter Harris, founder of A Rocha*

Ruth's love for the natural world bursts through every page of this book. For many years, she has shaped her life to share this planet with God's amazing community of creation. This book is a priceless handbook on how to live sustainably. Ruth does so humbly and honestly, sharing the joys and difficulties of being planet-friendly in a consumer's world.
*The Revd Margot Hodson, church minister, and Theology and Education Director, John Ray Initiative*

We are standing on the brink of ecological collapse. Many fall into the temptation of apathy or despair. In this inspiring book, Ruth Valerio moves us from apathy to action, challenging us with the urgent biblical mandate to become healers of the Earth. She moves us from despair into becoming drivers of change, not only by making individual lifestyle changes but also by becoming catalysts for significant transformation in society. This is a practical handbook of faith and action that every Christian should read, use and recycle by passing on to as many friends as possible!

*The Revd Dr Rachel Mash, Canon for the Environment, Anglican Church of Southern Africa*

I absolutely love this book. There cannot be a more poignant moment to pick such a relevant and engaging read. In these pages, we are invited to participate in a journey that will shape the future of our world and the world of so many others.

Ruth takes us on a journey which we can all engage in, with easy-to-access ideas and practices. I felt so energized, after having read this, to be part of that different story. Buying this book will change your life for the better and, in so doing, change our world.

*The Revd Mark Melluish, Pastor, St Paul's Church, Ealing, and Assistant National Leader, New Wine UK*

We rely on Ruth for her readiness to tell it as it is and urge us to action. We owe her much for the way she brings us back to our calling and responsibilities. This book takes us even further, offering a challenge that none of us can ignore. Buy it, read it and make a difference.

*Dr Elaine Storkey, theologian, author, speaker and social scientist*

# L

## IS FOR

# LIFESTYLE

### CHRISTIAN LIVING THAT
### DOESN'T COST
### THE EARTH

# L IS FOR LIFESTYLE

## CHRISTIAN LIVING THAT DOESN'T COST THE EARTH

## RUTH VALERIO

INTER-VARSITY PRESS
36 Causton Street, London SW1P 4ST, England
Email: ivp@ivpbooks.com
Website: www.ivpbooks.com

The publisher has endeavoured to ensure that the URLs for external websites mentioned in this book were correct and live when the book went to press. The publisher is not, however, responsible for the content of these websites and cannot guarantee that they will remain live or that their content is or will remain appropriate.

First published 2004
New edition 2008
Reprinted 2011
Revised and updated edition 2019

**British Library Cataloguing-in-Publication Data**
A catalogue record for this book is available from the British Library.

ISBN: 978–1–78359–996–7
eBook ISBN: 978–1–78974–101–8

Set in Dante 12/15pt

Typeset in Great Britain by CRB Associates, Potterhanworth, Lincolnshire
Printed in Great Britain by Ashford Colour Press Ltd, Gosport, Hampshire

*Inter-Varsity Press publishes Christian books that are true to the Bible and that communicate the gospel, develop discipleship and strengthen the church for its mission in the world.*

*IVP originated within the Inter-Varsity Fellowship, now the Universities and Colleges Christian Fellowship, a student movement connecting Christian Unions in universities and colleges throughout Great Britain, and a member movement of the International Fellowship of Evangelical Students. Website: www.uccf.org.uk. That historic association is maintained, and all senior IVP staff and committee members subscribe to the UCCF Basis of Faith.*

# CONTENTS

# ACKNOWLEDGMENTS

A Rocha was my home for the whole lifetime of this book in one way or another, and it remains a unique organization that combines hands-on practical conservation work with a deeply rooted biblical faith. And now I feel immensely privileged to be working for Tearfund – an organization that works through the church on the ground to tackle the root causes of poverty, respond to disasters and see people's lives transformed. Its achievements so far have been staggering, but there is a lot of work still to be done, and I am thrilled to be a tiny part of that.

I want to thank those people who have assisted with *L is for Lifestyle*. Roy McCloughry helped enormously with the very first manuscript, and I owe the original book to him and to Stephanie Heald, my then editor at IVP. Various people and organizations helped with the second edition, and I don't want them to be forgotten: my parents Martin and Elizabeth Goldsmith; Chris Davis from the Fairtrade Foundation; Dave Bookless from A Rocha; Bill Guyton from the World Cocoa

Foundation; Canon Edmund Newell from St Paul's Cathedral; Friends of the Earth and the Soil Association Information Services; Richard Hunter from Equity Invest; Duncan Green from Oxfam; Abby Dalglish from Banana Link; Nick Spencer from Theos; Professor John Chudleigh from Analysing Agriculture (Australia); and my editor then and now at IVP, Eleanor Trotter, who deserves a special mention for her commitment and help in seeing this book through to a third edition.

For this new edition, I have had an amazing army of volunteers helping with the research needed to bring everything up to date. I couldn't have done it without Jean Leston, in particular, who gave up an incredible amount of time to be my unofficial research assistant, and this book benefits not only from all her fact finding but also from her own personal wisdom and from having worked for WWF and being on the Board of Operation Noah. Alongside her, Rich Bull, Alicia Humphreys, Megan McAuley, Isaac Stovell and Bev Thomas have contributed to different chapters and been wonderfully generous with their time. I must also thank my Twitter and Facebook friends for all their creative suggestions and ideas when I've pinged up a question online!

Finally, of course, thanks to my wonderful family who make me who I am and have both allowed me to follow this particular passion that God has placed on my life and have joined in with the fun and challenges it has brought. I finished the Introduction to the original book saying of Mali and Jemba, 'May I inspire in them the love for God's world and his people that my parents inspired in me.' That continues to be my prayer.

# INTRODUCTION

I'm on the train coming back from twenty-four hours with all the ministers of a diocese in the North-West of England. We've had a great time together – 400 of us in the cathedral exploring the theme 'The Earth is the Lord's', and thinking through together how we can live that out, in our own lives and in our churches.

As part of a worship session I led during my teaching, I asked people to picture a place in nature where they meet God, or where God has spoken to them in the past. I asked them to picture themselves there – not as consumers of that place but as participants in the community of creation that was around them – and to ask God to give them a new love for that area. Then I asked them, slowly, to imagine zooming out of the picture to the wider area . . . the country . . . the world, and, as they did so, again to ask God to fill them with love for what they were seeing.

I wonder if you might do that too, as we begin this book. We know we live in a world with appalling, heartbreaking, shocking problems on both a human and an environmental level (though, as we will also see throughout the book, there is good news too), and all of us want to do something to help. Often life takes over, and the scale of the issues can seem overwhelming, leading to a sense of hopelessness and not knowing where to start. This book will help you think through what you can do, taking the big issues of the day and breaking them down into manageable, bite-sized chunks, giving very practical pointers as to how we can respond. And the motivation for doing that comes not from a sense of duty or responsibility, but out of love.

You may be new to these issues, but keen to learn more about what is happening and take some first steps. You may be doing lots already and need some fresh ideas. You may be a student wanting to know what lifestyle options you can adopt as you study and when you graduate. You may want to know how to juggle the demands of a young family and mortgage repayments and still be a Christian actively concerned with wider global issues. Perhaps you are well established in life, with children at university and a good income (and a matching credit card bill!) coming in every month, and yet you still want to know how to use the things God has blessed you with to bless others. You might now be retired, or maybe you have been made redundant, and you want to discover how to use your time to make a difference. Perhaps you are just exhausted with the pressures of consumerism and you want to explore the possibilities of a simpler lifestyle. You may even have read *L is for Lifestyle* when it was first published fifteen years ago, and you want to see what has changed and what more you can do!

There are many things we can do to make a difference, and this book gives suggestions for minor changes as well as major challenges. Whatever your situation, you will find things to encourage and inspire you. Conversely, your particular situation may also mean there are aspects of this book that you cannot take on. The aim is definitely not to make you feel guilty! Try taking a step-by-step approach, doing one or two things first, rather than taking on all the action points at once. When they become a part of your normal life, then do some more. This is a book to come back to again and again, dipping into different chapters as you wish.

It will be obvious as you read on that this book comes from my own journey. Towards the start of my adult life I became aware of the problems that our world was facing, and I decided that, as a follower of Jesus, I wanted to play my part in doing something about them, and so have spent the past twenty-five years or so trying to do just that. The book therefore arises from my own circumstances – that is, normal life! I don't live up a mountain in self-sufficiency; I live on a 'social housing' estate with a family, financial commitments and the stress of supermarket shopping. Lots of this book I am living already, and I hope I am an encouraging example of the fact that it can be done despite a busy and very full-on life. There are parts of this book, though, where the suggested action is still an aspiration for me. For those of you who know me well, I ask you to be kind! Because it comes from my own journey, this book contains a lot of my personal opinions and stories. There will no doubt be things you disagree with, or other ways of achieving the same ends. I hope you will find your own way through the pointers that this book provides.

It has been fascinating rewriting *L is for Lifestyle* some fifteen years on from when I first wrote it, and incredible to see what has changed. Can you imagine that back then I needed to explain what climate change was . . . there were no Fairtrade products in the supermarkets . . . I didn't mention emails when talking about taking campaign actions . . . no-one had a smartphone and I don't think I even had a mobile phone myself?! So many food and drink items have moved from luxury to everyday, and no-one bats an eyelid at clicking for something online and it being delivered the next day (in a disproportionately huge box of course). When this book was first published, Tony Blair was Prime Minister in the UK, and George W. Bush was elected into the White House. That fast pace of change is continuing alarmingly, and no doubt there will be elements of this book that become obsolete over time, and new issues that will arise, as has happened over the past fifteen years. Where that is the case, I hope still that *L is for Lifestyle* will equip you with principles and behaviour change that outlast outdated stats, and that you will develop what I would call an ethical instinct.

There is good news to be celebrated: overall, the world has become a better place for people to live in, and we have seen an amazing fall in poverty rates in recent decades. We should take that good news as encouragement that we really can make a difference. Nonetheless, we still face major challenges, many of which we will meet throughout the book. The fall from poverty has not been experienced equally around the world (it has happened mostly in China and Asia, with sub-Saharan Africa remaining in desperate need. Indeed, by 2030 90% of the world's poor will live in Africa), and environmental destruction and growing inequality could reverse that trend. And, as that rise out of poverty has happened, the world has become a much worse place for the non-human world. The Assessment Reports coming from the Intergovernmental Panel on Climate Change have left us in no doubt that climate change is real, is caused predominantly by human activity, and is impacting the world's poorest the most. There is an urgent need to slash our carbon dioxide ($CO_2$) (and methane) emissions in order to keep levels of warming below 1.5 degrees above pre-industrial limits if we are to prevent catastrophe. Alongside this, reports from the World Bank, Stockholm Resilience Centre, World Wildlife Fund and the UK-based Royal Society for the Protection of Birds, among many others, have all shown the devastating impacts of our human behaviour on the wider natural world.

I hope I don't give the impression in this book that all we need do is shop a bit more ethically and then we have 'done our bit'. Those of us who live in the wealthier segments of global society (wherever we live in the world) must be prepared to limit our lifestyles, and radically. In particular, with Europe and the US between them being responsible for more than 90% of the emissions that are already in the atmosphere, if we come from those parts of the world, we are surely the ones who have to make the most sacrifices.

Reading the Introductions to the two previous editions of this book has been an interesting trip down memory lane. I finished the original manuscript two weeks before daughter number two was born, and so these past fifteen years have been just as much about trying to do family life in an ethical way on a pretty limited income as they have been about my external speaking and writing and my commitment to help the church engage in caring for the whole creation.

Over these years, 'many little steps in the right direction' has become my motto, along with some big steps too. We gradually changed our eating habits, started up a pig cooperative that we did for ten years with about twelve other families (stopping only when our meat consumption became so little that it wasn't worth continuing, but having lots of fun learning about rearing happy, healthy animals and making our own bacon and sausages), and tried to produce our own food as much as possible, including growing veg and keeping chickens. Already with a green energy supplier before writing the first edition, we have since installed solar panels for both electricity and hot water, and I now have an electric car which I love and can charge from the panels when the sun is shining. Making a clear decision to reduce my plastic usage has led to an adventure in alternative cleaning and beauty products (liquid handwash and shower gel: possibly one of the biggest plastic-inducing cons in recent decades. Anyone heard of soap?!), including stopping using conventional shampoo and conditioner, and washing clothes with soapnuts or an eco egg.[1] I have become increasingly concerned about the impact of our clothing on both the environment and the people who share it, and so try to buy new clothes seldom but sustainably, and am delighted by what I can get in my local charity shops. We have also deliberately holidayed in the UK and flown very little as a family, though I confess that is a challenge I'm painfully wrestling with in my work with Tearfund.

The challenges of living fairly in our world today are immense, and the issues we face are complicated. Nonetheless, there is joy to be found along the way, particularly when we join with other people, and I pray that *L is for Lifestyle* will be a useful companion to you as you take your 'many little steps in the right direction'.

One final note about referencing. It will become evident that this book draws on an immense number of sources. To have included all of them in the actual book would have made it too unwieldy for something that aims to be accessible and readable. So the notes mostly have been kept for the times when I quote from a specific person or book (which generally come from the earlier editions), and you can find a full list of all the sources used at <https://ruthvalerio.net>.

## Note

1. For more on these, see the Green Living pages (Plastic-free hair care) at <https://ruthvalerio.net>.

# A IS FOR ACTIVISTS

One of my most memorable experiences is of visiting the Missionaries of Charity, Mother Teresa's order, in Addis Ababa, Ethiopia. In that city of incredible poverty, their call is to the very bottom of the heap: to those who are dying and have been abandoned by friends and family. Each morning, the sisters open their compound gates and bring in those who have been abandoned there overnight. The compound is divided into separate rooms for different illnesses, each room containing neat rows of dying people on iron beds – a very unnerving sight.

The sisters themselves follow a rigorous routine. Their day starts at 5 a.m. with a set rhythm: practical care for those they are looking after, personal prayer, times of rest and eating, and corporate prayer with the other sisters. Through this rhythm, they are given the necessary strength to face the day's demands.

Few of us are called to lead the life of these sisters. Yet all of us in different ways are called to be activists for God's kingdom. Just consider these well-known words from the Old Testament:

> Is not this the kind of fasting I have chosen:
> to loose the chains of injustice
>     and untie the cords of the yoke,
> to set the oppressed free
>     and break every yoke?
> Is it not to share your food with the hungry
>     and to provide the poor wanderer with shelter –
> when you see the naked, to clothe them,
>     and not to turn away from your own flesh
>             and blood? . . .
> If you do away with the yoke of oppression,
>     with the pointing finger and malicious talk,
> and if you spend yourselves on behalf of the hungry
>     and satisfy the needs of the oppressed,
> then your light will rise in the darkness,
>     and your night will become like the noonday.
> (Isaiah 58:6–7, 9b–10)

This passage is found in the final part of Isaiah, which describes what Alec Motyer calls 'the characteristics of a waiting people', a people seeking to live an obedient life while waiting for the Lord.[1] The previous verses (2–5) describe the kind of fasting that God rejects. It is fasting that tries to manipulate a response from God (cf. 1 Kings 18:16–29), but actually leads only to exploitation and fights. Instead of using the time freed up by fasting for meaningless rituals (verse 5), the time should be spent working towards a just society (verse 6), taking care of the needs of strangers and family members (verse 7), and ensuring that personal behaviour matches this social response (verses 9–10).

These are hardly passive words; it is impossible to do these things without active involvement in what is happening in the world around us. This book is aimed at helping all who want to spend ourselves on behalf of the hungry and satisfy the needs of the oppressed. We can be activists in many different ways, but whatever we do, we do it in order to partner with God in seeing God's righteousness and justice extended into our world.

So let us look further at why we should be activists.

First, we are to be activists *because activism is rooted in the heart and character of God himself,* as Father, Son and Holy Spirit. The Bible tells of a trinitarian God, actively involved with his people, working out his plans for the salvation of the whole world. One of the best expressions of God's character is in Psalm 146:

He upholds the cause of the oppressed
   and gives food to the hungry.
The LORD sets prisoners free,
   the LORD gives sight to the blind,
the LORD lifts up those who are bowed down,
   the LORD loves the righteous.
The LORD watches over the foreigner
   and sustains the fatherless and the widow,
   but he frustrates the ways of the wicked.
(Psalm 146:7–9)

God's salvation plans find their fulfilment in the active nature of Jesus, the Son, who came down to this Earth as a human being to restore and reconcile the world to God (Romans 8:19–21; 2 Corinthians 5:18–21; Ephesians 2:11–18; Colossians 1:19–20). The incarnation is the ultimate expression of God's compassion as he enters into his creation, taking on our sin and suffering. Jesus' life continues this demonstration of his compassion, and his twin emphasis on the poor and on proclaiming the good news is best captured in what many would see as his manifesto:

> The Spirit of the Lord is on me,
>> because he has anointed me
>> to proclaim good news to the poor.
> He has sent me to proclaim freedom for the prisoners
>> and recovery of sight for the blind,
> to set the oppressed free,
>> to proclaim the year of the Lord's favour.
> (Luke 4:18–19)

Jesus came in order that we 'may have life, and have it to the full' (John 10:10), and he accomplished this by his life, death and resurrection on our behalf.

Second, we are to be activists *because activism is the call that God has placed on us*. Those earlier words from Isaiah 58 make that clear, and so does Micah 6:8:

> He has shown you, O mortal, what is good.
>> And what does the LORD require of you?
> To act justly and to love mercy
>> and to walk humbly with your God.

And Proverbs 29:7:

> The righteous care about justice for the poor,
>> but the wicked have no such concern.

Indeed, the way in which the nation of Israel was established would demonstrate that God's people were to be different from those around them. One of the main ways was through their treatment of other people and the land that God had created.

They were to look after those who were vulnerable and unable to look after themselves (e.g. Exodus 22:22; Deuteronomy 10:18–19), and laws were established to prevent huge inequalities appearing (e.g. the laws against moving boundary stones, Deuteronomy 19:14; 27:17). The best-known of these laws are the Jubilee laws of Leviticus 25. These recognized that differences in material status would appear, but sought to ensure that limits were imposed. While a person could gain extra land and reap the benefits of the income it brought, that land was eventually to be returned to the original owner at the time of the Jubilee. Jubilee speaks of liberation and restoration. The foundation for these laws was the experience of Israel's suffering in Egypt and her covenant relationship with a God who has an active love for justice (e.g. Leviticus 25:39–43).

Jesus' parable of the Good Samaritan in Luke 10 in the New Testament similarly urges us to be actively involved with our neighbour. The question asked by the expert in the law is effectively: 'Who is my neighbour, whom I should love as myself?' Jesus turns the answer round so that the neighbour is the one doing the active caring (rather than the one who needs to be cared for, as is often presumed), and tells the 'expert': 'Go, then, and be that neighbour yourself.' There is no excuse allowed for knowing of someone's distress and doing nothing about it. James emphasizes this too when he stresses that the mark of a religion that is acceptable to God is that we 'look after orphans and widows in their distress and . . . keep [ourselves] from being polluted by the world' (James 1:27).

Just as the Israelites' experience of redemption was the foundation for their care of the poor, so it is Jesus' death for us that gives us the ultimate reason for our calling to be activists on behalf of those in need:

> This is how we know what love is: Jesus Christ laid down his life for us. And we ought to lay down our lives for our brothers and sisters. If anyone has material possessions and sees a brother or sister in need but has no pity on them, how can the love of God be in that person? Dear children, let us not love with words or speech but with actions and in truth.
>
> (1 John 3:16–18)

Third, we are to be activists *because we have been made in the image of God* (Genesis 1:26–27). This term has a number of facets to it (more of which we shall see in 'C is for Creation'). One important aspect is our creation as relational beings and our ability to have an intimate relationship with God. This is wonderfully captured by Augustine, who famously prayed in the opening sentences of his *Confessions*, 'You have made us for yourself, and our hearts are restless until they find their rest in you.' There is a God-focused dimension within us all that is integral to what it means to be human.

This is important in understanding why we should be activists in our world today. It is highlighted by the covenant that God made with Noah and all living creatures, which sees our creation in the image of God as the reason why we are accountable for one another (Genesis 9:5–6). So our relationship with God is extended to our relationship with one another. A person who is viewed as just a physical being, devoid of all spiritual orientation, is, in essence, dehumanized. When we lose our true humanity, we must search for it elsewhere; hence the rampant rise of materialism. When we lose our true humanity, we lose our basis for compassion and concern, and that is what leads to the terrible injustices in our world today.

Fourth, we should be activists *because of the state of our world*. In many ways the state of our world is improving, and huge steps have been taken in tackling poverty. This should encourage us that we *can* make a difference and see change – and let that knowledge motivate us to keep going. But we live in a world where still 15,000 children under the age of five will die today, mostly from poverty-related causes, and 800 of these will die of malaria, and 41% of the population of Africa live in extreme poverty, below $1.90 a day. In the UK, 14 million people live in poverty, and 13% of all nineteen-year-olds in England lack minimum levels of academic qualification. In the US, there are 28 million (8.8% of the population) with no health insurance. Each of these people has been made in the image of God, so how can we not be active in working to continue to see change?

And we live in a world in which there has been a 60% decline in the size of populations of mammals, birds, fish, reptiles and amphibians. Each of these creatures has been created by God and is loved by him, so how can we not be active in working to see change?

Finally, we are to be activists *because of our hope for the future*. The above statistics lead to a sombre recognition that the world is not as it should be and we shall never sort everything out in the present. The good news of Jesus is that we can look forward to a very different future, one that we begin to experience now through his life, death and resurrection, but that will be brought in fully when he comes again (Ephesians 1:13–14).

The final chapters of Revelation give us a picture of that future, when there will be 'no more death or mourning or crying or pain' (21:4), and when the river of the water of life will flow and the tree of life will bear fruit (22:1–2). It is this future hope that motivates us in our lives today, in the same way that Paul's teaching on the future led him to encourage us to live a godly life in the present (e.g. 1 Corinthians 15:58; 1 Thessalonians 4:13 – 5:11). In the words of Jürgen Moltmann, 'From first to last, and not merely in the epilogue, Christianity is eschatology, is hope, forward looking and forward moving, and therefore also revolutionizing and transforming the present.'[2]

As we live in the tension between the 'now' that Jesus' first coming has brought and the 'not yet' that will be realized with his second coming, we are to demonstrate an active attitude of 'eager anticipation' (Romans 8:19). Our role is to be living examples of the future, anticipating now what we know the future holds.

What sort of activists, then, should we be?

First, as the Missionaries of Charity so beautifully demonstrate, we should be prayerful activists. Prayer connects us with the people and situations around the world for whom and for which we are praying. It reminds us of our motivation: to see the kingdom of God manifest in our world. It reminds us that there is a strong spiritual dimension to all we do. Above all, prayer reminds us that we cannot do everything by ourselves or in our own power. Ultimately, we depend on God to bring his redeeming power to bear in the situations in which we work. Prayer also causes us to stop and take time for reflection. Activists are not action-junkies, and taking time to rest is a thoroughly biblical thing to do.[3]

Second, we should be knowledgeable activists. The problems that face our world are immensely complicated, and we must not be simplistic or naïve. Books, magazines, websites, newsfeeds, and TV and radio programmes will all provide helpful information. One of the best things we can do is join an organization that can give us the resources we need.

Third, we should be gracious and joyful activists. As I have discovered, it can be easy to become self-righteous and moralistic, preaching to others about where their lifestyle is wrong. Jesus made it clear that we must focus on our own failures first (Matthew 7:3–5). It may take all our lives to remove the plank in our own eyes before we can remove the speck from someone else's!

Being activists is what this book is about. The following chapters aim to give us knowledge and a way forward along this route.

## Action points

- Choose one thing that will build up your knowledge and understanding of some of the issues we shall be looking at in further chapters. For example, you could commit to watching the news regularly, sign up to *The Guardian* newspaper's weekly environment email, or look at the World Bank website, which has a wealth of information around poverty reduction and sustainability.
- As you do so, ask God to give you vision and fill you with Jesus' compassion.

## Notes

1. J. Alec Motyer, *The Prophecy of Isaiah* (IVP, 1999), pp. 461, 478–482.
2. Jürgen Moltmann, *Theology of Hope* (SCM Press, 2010), p. 2.
3. CAFOD, Christian Aid, Open Doors and Tearfund are among many organizations that produce helpful prayer material to help our prayers maintain a global focus.

# B IS FOR BANANAS

My eldest daughter loves bananas. When she was younger her grandma used to tell her that one day she would end up looking like one (you'll be pleased to know that hasn't happened). Indeed, bananas have become one of the basic foods that we all eat today: so basic that the banana is the world's most popular fruit, worth £6 billion in the UK ($8 billion in the US) a year, and around 90% of UK and US households buy them. We eat more bananas than we do apples; they bring a lot of profitability to both UK and US supermarkets.

Yet my parents' generation almost never ate them. Do we ever stop to think what has taken place in order for bananas to be such an ordinary part of our lives, rather than an exotic fruit that we rarely see? As commonplace as they may seem, bananas are the perfect way to introduce us to the big, complex game that is global trade. This is the story of the Banana Wars – and in particular the supermarket price wars.

Corporate power is very concentrated, with the multinationals (Chiquita, Dole and Del Monte, Fyffes and Noboa) and big UK/US supermarkets controlling production, and there is now a race to the bottom in terms of price. The price of bananas has fallen sharply from 18p per banana a decade ago to only 11p, and UK and US supermarkets try to keep bananas artificially cheap in order to attract shoppers and increase their market share. This means that the income of workers and small farmers is being badly squeezed. The heavy use of chemicals also continues, recently exacerbated by an outbreak of a fungal disease that affects Cavendish bananas (the main type we eat). Workers are increasingly fighting back, asking for fair minimum prices for bananas as well as health compensation.

One ray of hope that has emerged in the UK since the original version of this book was launched has to be the commitment of many supermarkets to buying Fairtrade bananas. But despite the growth of Fairtrade bananas in the UK, the overwhelming majority of those consumed globally are produced in bad conditions.

There are two main issues here. First, the plantation workers live in poverty. In the Dominican Republic, for example, the workers are paid an average of just $6.50 a day, and in Ecuador three-quarters of banana workers receive an income below the poverty line. Although the Ecuadorian government has set a minimum price for bananas of 10p per pound (454 g), many small farmers receive as little as 4p per pound, which does not even cover their costs.

On average, the non-Fairtrade worker gets only 5–9% of the price of a banana. As with many other commodities exported to the north, nearly 80% of the price stays with the multinationals and supermarkets, and is never seen by the producer.

Second, vast quantities of chemicals, including pesticides, are used to treat the bananas during their production. This poses a risk to banana workers and the surrounding environment. Banana plantations typically apply more than 35 lb (16 kg) of pesticides per acre, far more than the average for intensive farming in industrialized countries. In Costa Rica, most banana workers suffer health damage, such as skin lesions or respiratory problems. Their children are also badly affected by high concentrations of these chemicals in their bodies, causing brain damage, while tens of thousands of male workers across banana-exporting countries are sterile due to one of the toxic pesticides. In Ecuador, entire communities suffer from indiscriminate aerial crop spraying.

It will be no surprise to learn that many other foods are also produced and traded in ways that do great damage to the producers and the environment, such as chocolate, avocadoes, tea, sugar and rice, and also goods such as clothes, electronic products and children's toys. One commodity that I have got to know lots about over the past fifteen years is jewellery, and gold in particular. And the reality of what lies behind our jewellery is shocking. On average, for every 0.333 g gold ring that reaches the shops, 20 tonnes of toxic waste (cyanide or mercury) are created, and often washed into the rivers that local people depend on for their fresh water. More than 100 million people are dependent upon small-scale mining globally, earning an average daily wage of $2, making it a poverty-driven activity, the third biggest employer in the world after agriculture and textiles, and a massively important area in which to be working to bring about positive change (see <https://credjewellery.com> and <www.fairgold.org>).

It is a harsh reality that we are able to buy the things we do, at the prices we enjoy, because those who are making or producing them are not being paid a proper wage by the large companies that own them.

But are there alternatives, and is there anything we can do about it?

The answer is 'yes' to both questions.

There are three routes open to us. The first is Fairtrade. Fairtrade schemes cut out the middlemen and work directly with cooperatives and farmers' associations that are organized and governed so they are accountable to their members. They guarantee a fixed minimum price that covers the cost of sustainable production, providing a floor price that helps protect smallholders against fluctuations in commodity prices. On top of this, Fairtrade pays a premium to its worldwide producers, worth €150 million in 2016, that is invested into priority projects such as schools and health centres and business development. The Fairtrade scheme means there is a commitment on the part of the traders to engage in long-term trading relationships which provide greater income security, so helping the producers to invest in the future. In addition to this, traders commit to making finance available at market rates so that producer organizations can meet the demands of the contract, such as investment in seeds or tools, and so on.[1]

Since first writing this book, Fairtrade has exploded in the UK, with retail sales increasing from £32.9 million in 2000 to £1.6 billion in 2016. Fairtrade sales in the US have a long way to go to catch up, but they are also growing rapidly, worth over $1 billion in 2016. There are now more than 1.65 million farmers and workers participating in Fairtrade in seventy-four countries. In 1996, 2,500 of the world's 10 million sold bananas were Fairtrade, with none being available in the UK. In 2017, Fairtrade bananas made up 30% of the UK banana market, a figure boosted considerably by the decision of Sainsbury's,

Waitrose and the Co-op to buy only Fairtrade bananas. It is amazing to think that when I first wrote this book, Fairtrade chocolate wasn't available in the supermarkets (the first Fairtrade chocolate bar, Maya Gold, was launched one month after this book was published) – how much has changed!

Fairtrade tea and coffee are now widely available in coffee shops, both on the high street and on the station platform, and M&S, the Co-op and Waitrose now sell only Fairtrade tea. Many other supermarkets, including US chains such as Whole Foods, Trader Joe's and Walmart's Sam's Club, stock a wide range of Fairtrade coffee, chocolate, sugar, flowers, wine and other products. Worldwide, consumers spent €7.9 billion on Fairtrade-certified products in 2016, an increase of 847% from 2004.

If ever there is a case of consumer power, it is here, and I hope the story of Fairtrade's success will encourage and motivate you to support Fairtrade even more! There is always the temptation for companies to move away from it in favour of increasing profits (as seen in Cadbury's move away from Fairtrade chocolate, and Sainsbury's decision to reduce their support for Fairtrade tea in favour of their own 'fairly traded' brand), so we must continue to press for it.

One particular frustration of mine concerns Easter eggs, and the lack of Fairtrade chocolate used by the major companies. Every year I contact the supermarkets and ask them to stock more Fairtrade eggs. Please join me in doing the same, and maybe together we will make a difference!

Fairtrade (FT) is the ideal that must be striven for. The present reality, though, is that few companies can truthfully assert they know how all their goods are produced, since a typical supply chain is vast.

The second alternative route available to us, therefore, is to push, where FT is not yet an option, for ethical trade.

Ethical trade is about ensuring that minimum international labour standards are met. These standards include freely chosen employment; freedom to form trade unions; safe and hygienic working conditions; no child labour; payment of living wages; no excessive working hours; minimum environmental damage; and no discrimination. For these things to happen, companies need to be prepared to aim for longer-term solutions, improving supply chains through incremental changes. Most of the goods that we buy will not carry the FT label, but we can still play our part in encouraging companies to operate more ethically by becoming more educated and informed about the products we are purchasing, and asking questions of companies whenever we want to buy from them.

The good news is that knowledge and transparency have improved in recent years, with the growth in industry-led bodies developing more sustainable supply chains, for example, the Roundtable for Sustainable Palm Oil (RSPO) or Forest Stewardship Council (FSC), as more companies realize they need to demonstrate social and environmental responsibility in all aspects of the chain, in order to win consumer trust. The UN Global Compact, which gets heads of companies to commit to sustainability practices, has also published supply chain sustainability guidelines.

This has led to a number of other ethical certification/sourcing schemes besides FT, which we can support when FT isn't available, such as the Rainforest Alliance and supermarket ethical own-branding. Of course, this can make ethical decisions quite confusing, and I would always encourage you to do your own research into these schemes, as sometimes they don't offer as many benefits to the small farmer/worker as does Fairtrade.

Although we have a long way to go, I am encouraged by the growth of ethical consumer power in the US and UK, for all types of products (from food and drink to household products, cars, toiletries and clothing), since this book was first written. For example, average annual UK household expenditure on ethical products is now £1,263, more than double what it was in 2006. And 56% of Americans say they stop buying from companies they believe are unethical. This increase in demand is prompting more companies to provide the ethical products that people want. Consumer activism and boycotts have also increased (e.g. a Greenpeace-led campaign against Nestlé for using palm oil which causes harm to orangutans through habitat destruction, and a grassroots boycott of Starbucks for its treatment of Ethiopian coffee workers), forcing companies to rethink their policies. However, we need to keep up the pressure!

The third route is trade justice. One of the main ways in which a country can be lifted out of its poverty is through increasing its exports to the richer countries. The rules for international trade, however, are governed by the commercial and financial interests of those richer countries, and thus are shaped to their own advantage. These rules are enforced primarily through three institutions: the WTO, the International Monetary Fund and the World Bank.[2] Trade justice is about seeing a major overhaul to the current system so that the rules work for poor people rather than against them. This reform of the institutions would include such measures as making poverty eradication a key objective, ensuring a truly democratic and transparent process, and monitoring the activities of transnational corporations as well as of governments. One of the key shifts I have seen happen over recent years is an increasing recognition of the vital role of international bodies in achieving development goals, for example, implementing the UN Sustainable Development Goals (SDGs) in areas such as poverty reduction, education, health and the environment. When I first became interested in issues around justice, poverty and the environment, the World Bank was seen as the enemy, and huge pressure was brought to bear on it (and on the WTO and the IMF) to reform. Now the World Bank states its existence as being to 'fight poverty worldwide through sustainable solutions' and it is working positively in many places. Within such a large institution there are inevitably varying degrees of commitment to its stated goal, and varying views as to how best to get there, but reform of these bodies *is* happening through international pressure for trade justice. We need to keep up this pressure (e.g. Tearfund ran a successful campaign calling on the World Bank to put more of its energy funding into renewable energy projects), and be encouraged that, as citizens and consumers, we can be using our voices to call for these changes to take place.[3]

With so many avenues open to us, we can begin playing our part in changing, for the good, the lives of the people who grow or make the things we buy. We have already seen how Jesus' parable of the Good Samaritan teaches us that we are to be neighbours to those whom others ignore, and this applies to those living next door and those on the other side of the world. Through taking the time and trouble to buy fairly traded products, and by getting involved in working for a fairer and more ethical trading system, we can take a step towards being that neighbour ourselves.

**Action points**

- Increase your awareness of the issues behind the products you buy. Take time to ask retailers where the product comes from and whether they have looked into the conditions of the producers. For more information on food and supermarkets, see 'F is for Food'.

- If there is a Fairtrade option for the product you are buying, buy it! This will often mean being prepared to pay a higher price. If you find this hard to swallow, tell yourself that you are paying the price you should be paying anyway and are stopping others from getting ripped off.
- Consider setting up a Fairtrade stall at your place of work or worship. That way, you and others can gain access to a greater number of fairly traded goods than the supermarkets provide.
- Find out more about the Trade Justice Movement and consider how you might get involved.

## Notes

1. For more details, see <www.fairtrade.org.uk>.
2. There is not the space here to look in detail at how these organizations are set up and run. For more information, see Jospeh E. Stiglitz, *Globalization and Its Discontents Revisited: Anti-Globalization in the Era of Trump* (W. W. Norton & Co., 2017), and the excellent resources that can be obtained from Global Justice Now, Tearfund, Oxfam and Christian Aid. See also the relevant websites: <www.wto.org>; <www.imf.org>; <www.worldbank.org>.
3. The Trade Justice Movement gives us the opportunity to do exactly that. It is a coalition of organizations campaigning to see these changes take place so that trade can work for everyone. It brings together aid agencies, environment and human rights campaigns, FT organizations, and faith and consumer groups. For more information, see <www.tradejusticemovement.org.uk>.

# C IS FOR CREATION

Some years ago I made a beautiful tapestry that I love very much. It's a William Morris design of a peacock in the woods and it hangs proudly on the wall. In fact, I'm looking at it as I write this chapter.

Can you imagine how I would feel if I came home one day to find that Mali and Jemba had put it on the floor and were wiping their muddy feet on it? I'd be horrified . . . devastated . . . so upset! Well, I can tell you with complete certainty that would never happen. Why? Because they love me and wouldn't dream of doing something so terrible to something I value so much! And they love it too, because I love it.

The point is obvious, isn't it? In Genesis 1:31 we are told that God looked at what he had made and said, 'It is very good.' It's fantastic! This world is amazing! This world is God's creation, and he loves it. So therefore don't we also want to love it and look after it? How does God feel when we wipe our ecological footprints all over it and leave it damaged and wrecked?

'C is for Creation' is one of my favourite chapters in this book (you'll have to guess which my other ones are). Over the years, I have become increasingly convinced just how important God's creation is to him – not only the human part of his creation, but the *whole* of it – and that living in a way that takes care of that creation is an absolutely fundamental part of what it means to follow Jesus, as integral to our Christian faith as evangelism and reading the Bible, helping people in poverty and praying. When I look in the Bible, I see four basic reasons as to why that is.

First, as we have already seen, *because God made this world and he loves it.*

Some theologies have promoted muddled notions of a separation between body and spirit, earth and heaven, natural and spiritual: exalting the latter and denigrating the former, so that nature / creation is thought to be inferior to the 'supernatural' realm. In contrast to this, the world carries within it the intrinsic value of something that God has made and finds pleasure in – and note that God pronounced creation 'good' before humanity was created. Because he has made it, it belongs to him, first and foremost (Psalm 24:1). While we are called to be his representatives (Genesis 1:26–30), it is only through his continual influence that the Earth is sustained. One of the key biblical principles arising out of this is that the right of all to use the Earth's resources comes before anyone's right to ownership. The Earth, then, has been given to us not as something that God no longer cares about, but as a gift that we are to treasure and look after (Genesis 2:15).

Second, *God has created us to look after the rest of his creation.*

In the Old Testament the idea of dominion is used of the Hebrew kings, and embodies within it the idea of 'servant kingship', reflecting God's own kingly rule within creation, which is undoubtedly a caring and providing one rather than one of domination. Genesis 1:26–28, however, has caused problems in the church through a misunderstanding of the words 'dominion' and 'subdue', and hence a misunderstanding of the account of creation as a whole. This has led some to an anthropocentric view of creation that holds that everything revolves around humanity, and was made for our benefit. It is certainly true that there is a distinction between human beings and the rest of creation: as we will see in a moment, we are the only ones to have been made 'in the image of God'. Because of this distinction between humanity and the rest of creation, the psalmist can describe humanity as being a little lower than the heavenly beings (or God), and crowned with glory and splendour, and as having the rest of God's creation 'under their feet' (Psalm 8:5–6).

But we have too often failed to remember that we are a part of creation, and not separate from and superior to it. It is an inescapable fact that we are part of the same ecosystems and structures that form the rest of creation. In fact, as the Old Testament scholar Dr Chris Wright states, the opening chapters of Genesis 'do not immediately emphasize human uniqueness. On the contrary, it seems that at point after point we have more in common with the rest of the animate creation than in distinction from it.'[1] We might even question the popular interpretation that sees humanity as the climax of creation, since a less human-centred approach would see the real consummation and goal of creation as God's rest on day seven, which reminds us that all creation exists for God, to worship him, rather than for humanity.

Of immense significance in the creation narrative is the description of humanity as being made 'in God's image'. We began to explore what this phrase means in 'A is for Activists'.

One meaning that the author of Genesis particularly highlights is to do with the role that we are given regarding the rest of creation. Indeed, Chris Wright makes the point that the grammar used in Genesis 1:26–28 indicates that this is one of the main reasons why humanity is so made: 'because God intended this last-created species, the human species, to exercise dominion over the rest of his creatures, for that reason God expressly and purposefully creates this species alone in his own image.'[2] The sense of the verses could then be read as 'Let us make human beings in our own image and likeness, *so that* they may look after the rest of creation.'

'The image of God' carries the idea of being God's representative on earth, in the same way that physical images of a king would be set up throughout his territory to signal his lordship. By making humans in his image, God has given us delegated authority over his creation (*The Message* version talks about us being 'responsible for . . .'). It goes without saying that we should exercise that authority in a way that reflects his character, not through brutality and carelessness, but with love and compassion and service. Once I had understood the meaning of 'the image of God' in this way, it transformed my outlook. Suddenly I realized that the wider creation isn't here to serve me. Rather, it's the reverse: one of the main reasons why I am here is to look after the rest of what God has made. That was, and still is, exciting, humbling and challenging.

Third, *the world has gone wrong because of us.*

Our representation of the image of God, however, has been marred by the fall, because humanity turned away from God and people chose to go their own way. The fall broke humanity's relationship with God, with other humans, and with the rest of creation (see Genesis 3), which would now carry within itself the curse of God, as well as his blessing.

All through the Old Testament we see that the people's relationship with the wider natural world is important, and it matters how the land and all its inhabitants are treated. For example, the laws of the Sabbath apply more widely than only to humans (Leviticus 25), and a mother bird sitting on her nest is not to be taken (Deuteronomy 22:6). Interestingly, meat eating is only allowed after the fall and the story of Noah, and seems to reflect the reality of the people's sin (Genesis 9:1–3). The state of the land acts as a spiritual barometer for the health of the Israelites' relationships with God and with one another: where the people have turned away from God and aren't looking after other people, then the land responds accordingly and there is environmental upheaval (e.g. Deuteronomy 30:15–16; Jeremiah 5:23–25; Amos 8).

So the world has gone wrong because of us, and therefore we have a responsibility to put it back to rights again. But the good news is that we don't do that on our own or in our own strength – we do it as part of the mission of God and his plans for salvation because . . .

Fourth, *God has a future for this world.*

Our relationship with the rest of creation finds its centre in the coming of Jesus to live on earth as a human being, to die and be raised to life again. God's plan finds its fulfilment in Jesus, who affirms creation by choosing to become a part of that creation, and, by dying and being raised to life again and ascending into heaven with his resurrected body, brings potential healing to every broken relationship (Romans 8:19–22; 2 Corinthians 5:18–21; Ephesians 2:11–18). It is crucial to understand that God's intention for salvation involves the whole of creation, not just humanity alone (see also Colossians 1:15–20).

Revelation 4 is a stunning vision of the whole of creation, including human beings, worshipping the Lord God Almighty.

This is the end for which we have been made: to worship God completely and to enable the rest of creation to be made perfect in order to praise its Creator. This is a great privilege and also an awesome responsibility.

The Bible ends with a wonderful picture of the renewed heaven and the renewed earth (Revelation 21 – 22). This picture describes how the world that God has made as the new Jerusalem comes down from heaven – we do not 'go up there'. All things are made anew in Jesus, involving all creation, as the tree of life bears its fruit for all humanity to enjoy and the curse of the fall is finally ended. In a manner similar to our own resurrected bodies, there is both discontinuity (seen in 2 Peter 3:3–16) and continuity (seen in Romans 8:18–30) between the present and the new heaven and earth.[3] The emphasis of the word 'new' is on transformation rather than destruction, indicating 'newness in terms of quality rather than of something new that has never been in existence'. In this way, as Richard Bauckham and Trevor Hart say, we understand 'the new creation itself not as a replacement for the present world, but as the eschatological [relating to end times] future of this world'.[4]

This spurs us on to action. In 'A is for Activists' we saw how our future hope gives us the motivation for how we live today, in active expectancy and anticipation. Just as the incentive for our lives is to be seeing God's kingdom brought into this world now, so too, no less, with the rest of creation: it is our future hope that inspires us to work for its present, albeit partial, realization. This, for me, is what gives me my motivation for life, and for doing the things that I do: I want to live my life in such a way that I am building into that eschatological future when the whole of creation will be able to praise its Maker fully, rather than doing things that work against it.

So what does that mean for us?

First, we need to be learning about the major threats to God's creation: issues such as climate change, deforestation, the loss of species and biodiversity, consumer waste and pollution. We shall be exploring all of these and more in later chapters.

Second, we can then begin to consider what we can do in our own lives to start making a difference. When looking at such huge problems, it can be helpful to see ourselves standing within concentric circles, each circle representing a wider area for involvement. These areas are: ourselves, our church, our local community, our country and our world.

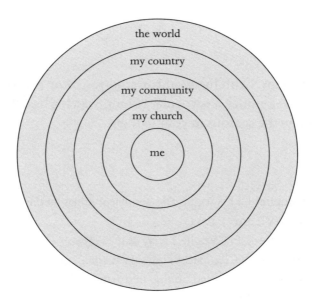

So, for example, we can change some of the everyday things we do, such as eating a more plant- and grain-based diet or reducing our car usage. In our churches the best thing we can do is take a look at Eco Church, which will give us all the tips and help we need. In our local communities there may be a conservation organization or environmental group we could join. Perhaps we could encourage our local authorities to improve recycling facilities. When we move on to our country and world, we begin to enter the area of campaigning. Here it is useful to belong to a national or international organization that will help us. (We will look more closely at these issues in later chapters.)

What we have to remember is that we cannot do everything. But that is no reason to do nothing! While each little action we take *is* only a drop in the ocean, together those drops will make a difference. Not only is this our responsibility; it is a part of the essence of being people created by God that we care for the rest of what he has created.

### Action point

- Fall in love with the world around you. Stop to smell a flower, notice a particular colour, watch a bird fly, follow the seasons in your garden . . .

### Notes

1. Christopher J. H. Wright, *Old Testament Ethics for the People of God* (IVP, 2010), p. 117.
2. Christopher J. H. Wright, *Living as the People of God: The Relevance of Old Testament Ethics* (IVP, 1984), pp. 82–83.
3. This is of course based on the 'first fruits' of Jesus' resurrection body, which demonstrates both continuity and discontinuity with his old body, and is both physical and spiritual, as he eats fish yet walks through walls.
4. Richard Bauckham and Trevor Hart, *Hope against Hope: Christian Eschatology at the Turn of the Millennium* (Eerdmans, 1999), p. 137.

# D IS FOR DRIVING

We've all seen the TV advertisements: just you, in your car, driving along an empty road. To drive a car is the stuff that life is made of. You are in control; you have the money and the look; you have the power to make your life whatever you want it to be. In a world of confusion and instability, your car is the one thing you can rely on: a safe haven from life's storms. Your car is, indeed, a car to be proud of.

There is no doubt that the car has brought many benefits. It is convenient to hop in and nip to the shops. In winter it is more comfortable, and in our busy lives driving saves so much time. It increases our employment options, allowing us to take a job some distance away, and helps us keep in touch with our scattered family and friends.

It is amazing to think how, over the course of just a few decades, our lifestyles have become so dependent on the car. There are over a billion cars in the world, and nearly 80 million new cars are made each year. (When I wrote this book's first edition fifteen years ago, that figure was 29 million new cars each year, so there has been a staggeringly huge increase!) Of the world's cars, 35% are owned by Americans and the fifteen wealthiest EU countries (one-tenth of the world's population), and if you think of China as a nation of bicycles, think again: China now has more cars (135 million) than any other country. In the UK the car is used for more and more shorter journeys. Forty per cent of car trips are under two miles long (up from 25% fifteen years ago), and 60% are under five miles. In the US in 2017, passenger cars covered 2,105,882,000,000 miles! Motor vehicles now produce nearly a quarter of $CO_2$ emissions in the US and the UK.

As we look at these statistics, it does not take much imagination to realize that, whatever the benefits, our car-dependent culture is also bringing with it great costs. The first cost is to ourselves. The emissions from a car consist of carbon monoxide, $CO_2$, lead, nitrogen dioxide, benzene, hydrocarbons and particulates. None of these is good for our health! Indeed, benzene is a known cancer-causing chemical, and it is no coincidence that the UK has one of the highest rates of asthma in Europe. Road traffic emissions, which have been falling since 1990 in the UK thanks to strict EU standards, are still the main source of UK air pollution, and constitute 20% of carbon monoxide emissions. Particulates from diesel exhausts are a particularly worrying problem, contributing to lung disease and poor air quality in cities. Interestingly, tests show that, in heavy traffic, children sitting in the back seat of a car are exposed to pollution levels nine to twelve times higher than outside. A recent study in California showed that air traffic pollution can result in DNA damage to children. In contrast to the health problems caused by driving, an adult who cycles regularly shows the fitness level of a person ten years younger rather than that of a non-cyclist of the same age.

The problem is even worse in other parts of the world. According to CNN, breathing the air in Delhi is the equivalent of smoking forty-four cigarettes a day because of the high level of particulates. In Mexico City the situation is so serious that a portion of residents' cars are banned on two weekdays per week, and two Saturdays per month, with each car being identified by a number on the registration plate.

In addition, the increase in car usage has had a dramatic impact on our communities. Parents are afraid to let their children walk to school or play outside because of the traffic. This is understandable when you consider that the second most common cause of death for school-age children is road accidents. A DfT National Travel Survey (2015) showed that walking to school is at its lowest-ever level. Only 48% of primary school children walk to school, compared to 70% in the 1970s. A Living Streets survey (2016) found that fear of dangerous traffic is the main reason why parents drive their children to school. But 82% of parents supported greater use of schemes to make it easier and safer for children to walk to school.

It is interesting too that car ownership is one of the main indicators of the increasing inequality to be found in the UK. About a quarter of households do not have a car, yet town planning and design favour those who own cars, with their emphasis on out-of-town shopping centres. People without cars are forced to shop in the smaller, local shops where goods are more expensive. We have seen already how the Old Testament laws, such as the Jubilee, sought to limit the inequalities that existed between people. For Christians, the improvement of access for all is an issue of equality and justice, and we should seize any opportunity to campaign for better-quality public transport, and for policies that keep our town centres vibrant.

The second cost is to the environment. We shall look at climate change later, but it is relevant to note here that $CO_2$ emissions from cars are continuing to rise, making transport the biggest contributor of $CO_2$ emissions in the UK economy (for the first time). Added to this is the impact that road building can have on precious wildlife sites, and on the lives of millions of animals.

Our petrol comes from the oil that is often carried in sea tankers. There have been several well-publicized and horrific oil disasters, not least that of Deepwater Horizon, possibly the biggest oil spill in US history, off the Gulf of Mexico. This 2010 disaster may have caused permanent damage to coastal salt marshes, as well as killing vast numbers of birds, dolphins, turtles and fish, and damaging coral reefs. Up to 800,000 sea birds alone died as a result of this spill.

Does it really have to be like this? The answer, of course, is no, but we have to be willing to do things differently. A number of cities across Europe and the US and Canada are having car-free days, introducing congestion charges, encouraging car sharing and installing EV charging points (the Scottish city of Dundee is a good example of this). Madrid has seen its residents' daily car usage drop by 6%, and in Paris in 2014 when they had a car ban, pollution levels dropped by 30%.

As I mentioned in the Introduction, one of the biggest changes I've made in recent years is to switch to a fully electric car. (If you're interested in the detail, I haven't bought it outright; I have it on a monthly lease, which makes it more feasible financially.) I made the change when I got my job with Tearfund and realized I would have to drive into the office much more than when I was with A Rocha. As a result, Tearfund installed charging points, which soon encouraged other colleagues to make the switch. I absolutely love driving an electric car (it is so smooth!), and it feels great to know that when I am charging it at home, the electricity is coming either from a renewable energy company (as is the case at Tearfund too), or for free from the solar panels on the roof.

One of the exciting and huge changes that we will see in the coming years is the wholesale move to electric, as sales of petrol and diesel cars will be banned in the UK from 2040 (and that date may well be brought forward). Developing the infrastructure for this is a big challenge, and it needs to be accompanied by an increase in renewable energy for charging the batteries. But the change is happening, and we need to jump on board: according to the International Energy Agency (IEA), there will be 50 million EVs on the roads by 2025, and 300 million by 2040.

What else can we do to make a difference?

A lot of this is about changing our attitudes. In the US and the UK, we have got so used to driving short distances that the thought of walking or cycling is not a pleasant one; it is so much more *convenient* to drive. We are cocooned in a culture that sees inconvenience as one of the greatest evils, to be avoided at all costs, and so we confuse what we perceive to be a need with what is actually just a nuisance: 'It takes more trouble to cycle or walk, therefore I need to drive.' But my mum used to cycle eight miles to school and back every day, even in the rain or the snow. That was nothing amazing – it was just what you did. I sometimes think of that if I am feeling that I would rather drive the 1.5 miles to the leisure centre!

What I have found is that what began as a discipline many years ago is now a pleasure. I now love to walk or cycle. I love the fact that I am outside, that I am not damaging God's creation in any way. I love the fact that I am getting some exercise; that it gives me space to pray; that I am more aware of what the seasons are doing; that I can appreciate the flowers in people's gardens and the birds in the hedges; that I can say hello to people from my neighbourhood and stop for a chat. I love the fact that my daughters have grown up without the impression that all journeys have to be made in a car (although I have to own up to the fact that this is still a contentious issue!).

Realistically, many of us will want to own and use a car, but there are still many things we can do here to make a difference. Always look for ways to car-share: if you know of someone else going to the same place as you, phone them up and offer a lift. When driving, keep your speed down. Driving at 50 mph uses 25–30% less fuel than driving at 70. I had to do this gradually. Many years ago I used to drive on the motorway at 80 mph (and felt virtuous for keeping my speed down to that!). When I began learning about the environmental costs, I decided to slow down. To jump from 80 mph to 60 was painfully frustrating, so I weaned myself off, five miles at a time: driving at 75 mph until that felt normal, then down to 70, and so on. For years now, I have left home a bit early and driven at 55 to 60, even on long journeys. Yes, it is aggravatingly slow, but you do get used to it, and the benefits to the environment and to your purse are worth it! Alongside that, being aware of the road ahead, and braking or accelerating gently, reduces your fuel consumption significantly.

Keeping your car in good condition improves efficiency. You can cut your driving emissions by regularly cleaning air filters, checking your oil, using less air conditioning, not idling your engine, checking your tyre pressure regularly, and using cleaning agents or better fuels (such as premium petrol) which help to remove dirt from the engine.

Finally, we must make sure we do not fall into the trap of thinking that if we are being more environmentally sensitive with our cars, it is OK to drive them more! Every time a car is started up, the world God made is damaged in some way. Sadly, every little trip to the supermarket contributes to climate change and pollution. As we saw in the previous chapter, the way we treat our world is a fundamental part of what it means to be a Christian. Someone once said to me that to be a disciple of Jesus and knowingly to harm his creation is a contradiction in terms. That is a sobering thought in relation to the amount we drive. So let's drive in a way that does the least damage possible, and, whenever we can, leave that car at home!

**Action points**

- Stop using your car for all short distances (and be prepared to lengthen your idea of a short distance!).
- If you have a bicycle, get it serviced so that it is in good condition, and invest in waterproof trousers.
- Drive more slowly.
- Do a 'car-fast' for a week and see what happens.

# E IS FOR ENERGY

The first thing I did this morning was wake up and have a shower. The water was hot and the house warm, thanks to our gas central heating. I then made myself a cup of tea and sat in bed, listening to my daily Bible reflection on my phone. I went downstairs for breakfast: toast made in the toaster from bread made in the bread machine, and muesli with soya milk kept cold in the fridge. I am now sitting here writing, listening to the radio, with a light on overhead. One good thing is that it looks set to be a sunny day, which means our solar panels will provide enough electricity to do a clothes wash, run the dishwasher and meet our electricity needs for the sunlight hours. (I'm looking forward to when I'll have a battery to store the unused electricity – that can't be too far away, I'm sure.)

All the things I have done so far required energy in the form of gas, petrol or electricity. I have done nothing out of the ordinary, but already I have used a good amount of energy.

Even the water I am drinking has been through an energy-intensive process to rid it, among other things, of the chemicals put in it by industry and agriculture, and from the cleaning products we use. The society we have created is totally dependent on using large amounts of energy in order to survive.

Over 80% of the energy that is used globally comes from the fossil fuels oil, coal and gas (with the rest coming from nuclear, hydro, biomass and renewables, including solar, wind and geothermal), and the problems associated with them are colossal.

At the forefront, of course, is climate change. This has become so much a part of our cultural language now that it can be easy to forget what those two words actually mean. The reality of it was brought home to me when I spent the day with Daniel on his *shamba* (smallholding) in central Tanzania, one of the countries being hardest hit by climate change. He was working hard to develop his small farmstead, but his land was dying. The fruits on his papaya and mango trees were not growing properly. His cashew nuts were not swelling as they should have been and his piglets were skinny. Daniel had planted a whole field of chilli plants, but they had all withered and died. The rains were late, and with each passing day the situation got worse.

When I first began writing and talking about climate change, I used to speak about the future and what scientists were predicting it would look like with a warming world: extreme weather events of flooding and droughts, rising sea levels, millions of species lost, millions of refugees, coral reefs dying, and a situation in which the poorest people and nations would be most affected. I have seen all that become a present reality, and it sickens me to the core that we have known about this for decades and done so little –

governments, businesses, churches and, yes, we ourselves as individuals.

While we can rejoice in the huge advances we have made towards ending extreme poverty, we have failed to do the same with climate change, and this could therefore undo much of the good done in lifting people out of poverty. A 2017 report from UN agencies showed that levels of hunger had risen for the first time since the turn of the century – because of climate change and conflict.

Oil is central to all this, as it is at the heart of every aspect of our global economy. Its extraction causes environmental degradation, and this is worsening with the growth of non-conventional types of oil such as tar sands and shale gas. Easy-to-reach oil reserves are disappearing, so oil companies are increasingly having to drill in difficult (deepwater) or pristine (e.g. Arctic) places to produce oil. Or they are extracting fossil fuels from non-conventional, hard-to-reach sources. Tar sands produce 20% more $CO_2$ than oil, and while fracking is less harmful than mining coal, it is still creating localized environmental problems and, overall, keeps us on a fossil fuel path that we need to move away from.

Because of its central place in the global economy, oil ('black gold') is a major factor in world politics. As leading environmental ethicist Professor Michael Northcott states, 'There is a very clear association between oil extraction, violent conflict and war.'[1] The first Gulf War was waged mainly because of the West's need to access Kuwait's oil, and many believe it was also a major factor in the Iraq War.

How do we regard what God has created? Our environmental crisis is, at its heart, a spiritual issue, linked with humanity's sin. Idolatry is central to our world: the false gods of wealth, power and security are worshipped in the place of the one true God. The environmental problems associated with our current use of fossil fuels can be attributed to human greed and selfishness; to our consumer society, which expects an ever-increasing standard of living; to an economic system that demands growth at any cost; and to government reluctance to invest heavily in renewables, influenced by the strong lobbying power of oil companies, resulting in significant political influence, especially in the US.

Our use of energy reflects our inability to imagine living any other way. However, our societies must wean themselves off the dependency on fossil fuels, and we must keep in the ground the majority of our remaining oil supplies and not burn them. Some cite nuclear power as an alternative, which already supplies the UK with 20% of its energy. Primarily, this is because nuclear power has very low $CO_2$ emissions. However, safety scares, the real cost of nuclear power and the lack of a solution to the problem of nuclear waste are distinct drawbacks. The real financial cost can be seen in the £30 billion subsidy for building Hinkley Point C, which will largely be paid for by consumers. These huge subsidies for nuclear power come at a time when UK government subsidies for solar power have been slashed by 87%, and there will be no new subsidies for green energy projects until after 2025. In the US, government subsidies for renewables have also been falling, by more than 50% since 2013. Some feel that, at least in the short term, nuclear power is necessary. But the debate continues.

There is some good news though! In recent years we have seen a dramatic shift away from coal (at least in the UK – the US has several coal-fired power stations still in operation, a key political issue, with the US coal industry receiving support from President Trump). The Drax B power station in Yorkshire, which in my earlier editions I said emitted more $CO_2$ into the atmosphere than the combined carbon emissions of Kenya, Malawi, Mozambique, Tanzania, Uganda and

Zambia, has now largely switched from burning coal to biomass, cutting its coal consumption by 70% between 2011 and 2017. The date 21 April 2017 was significant, as it was the first day since the 1880s that Britain didn't use coal to generate electricity.

This move away from coal has been accompanied by a big leap in renewables in both the US and UK, despite the government subsidy cutbacks, with the UK now getting nearly 30% of its energy from renewables at the time of writing. This has primarily been the result of the falling cost of renewable energy, especially solar (making it more competitive with fossil fuels), and improved renewable technology. Although the US is way behind at 17%, it is still staggering to note that solar energy now employs more people in the US than coal, oil and gas combined.

There is also good news politically, as there has been a growing sense of the urgency of climate change as a major world threat. In response to this, at the Paris climate conference (COP 21) in December 2015, 195 countries adopted the first-ever universal, legally binding global climate deal. This agreement set out a global action plan to put the world on track to prevent dangerous climate change by limiting global warming to well below 2°C, and provides a benchmark to hold governments and companies to account. Subsequent COP meetings have moved the benchmark to below 1.5. Before this, the UK made history in 2008 when it voted through the world's first Climate Change Act. This set a target to reduce emissions significantly by 2050 and a path as to how to get there, and established the Committee on Climate Change as an independent body holding the government to account on its targets. The government now needs to build on that and create an action plan for the UK to become net zero in its emissions by 2030.

So what are the areas in which we can begin to play our part? First, since **transport** is the fastest-growing source of $CO_2$ emissions, and accounts for 28% of US commercial and residential emissions and 34% of a British resident's household emissions, everything we looked at in our previous chapter applies here too: reduce car usage. Of course, cars are not the only issue: the environmental costs of both flying and food transportation must also be considered. We will look at these again in subsequent chapters.

Second, since a lot of $CO_2$ emissions in the UK and the US come from our **houses**, much energy saving is possible. We can use low-energy and LED light bulbs, insulate our homes effectively and wash our clothes on cooler temperatures, with full loads. Interestingly, the production of 'disposable' nappies uses far more energy than the laundering of washable ones. We should turn all appliances off standby, and buy the maximum energy efficiency-rated appliances when replacing. If everyone boiled just the amount of water needed in the kettle instead of filling it up, enough energy would be saved to power the whole of the UK's streetlights for the following night. Most importantly, we can reduce the amount of energy we use for heating and hot water. Turning the thermostat down by just 1°C, or using one hour less heating a day, can save 10% on fuel bills, while showering uses a quarter of the water of a bath. (For lots more ideas, see the section on 'An ecological concern' in my *Just Living: Faith and Community in an Age of Consumerism*, Hodder & Stoughton, 2016, and the Green Living pages on my website, <https://ruthvalerio.net>.) As we do these things, we will reduce our energy bills, demonstrating that self-interest and global responsibility really can go hand in hand!

Third, we can actively promote the use of **renewable energy** by switching to a 'green' electricity supplier (such as

Good Energy or Ecotricity) or going on to a 'green' tariff with our existing one. It is very easy to make the switch, and often doesn't cost any more. Encourage your church to do the same through the Big Church Switch, <www.bigchurchswitch.org.uk>. And, of course, if possible, then getting our own renewable energy at home is a great way to go.

Fourth, we can reduce the amount of **meat** and **dairy** we eat. This might come as a surprise, but we shall see in the next chapter that, globally, meat and dairy production contributes a large amount to climate change, and so switching to a predominantly vegetable and grain-based diet, or going fully vegetarian or vegan, is a key thing that we should all do (unless our health dictates otherwise).

Finally, last but not least, we can **ask our MPs** to put pressure on the government to provide more support for renewable energy and energy efficiency, to create policies that will reduce the UK's $CO_2$ emissions, and to play its part in implementing the Paris Agreement and persuading other countries to act similarly.

### Action points

- Decide on five ways in which you will reduce the amount of energy you use around the home. When you are doing these five easily, choose another five. If you live with your family, try to include them by asking them to imagine ways of reducing energy.
- Switch your electricity (and gas) to a green supplier.
- Get involved in the Climate Coalition, <www.theclimatecoalition.org>, and support Christian organizations and campaigns that are advocating political and personal action on climate change.

## Note

1. Michael Northcott, *A Moral Climate: The Ethics of Global Warming* (Orbis Books, 2007), pp. 49, 96.

# F IS FOR FOOD

I am obsessed with food. There are no two ways about it: food is the subject I will talk about most passionately and in which I have had the most amount of fun experimenting, finding different ways of doing things that are kind to both people and planet. So what has happened to cause this obsession in me? I blame it all on the innocent boxes of organic vegetables that have been coming into our house every week for the past twenty years, grown just a few miles away by the amazing Howard and Debbie of Veg Out, <https://vegoutorganic.co.uk>.

To begin with, I really disliked the scheme, but did it because I felt I ought to. The vegetables were often dirty, needing a good soak and a scrub, taking up precious time. I found the seasonal aspect of it frustrating, and I disliked the vegetables' blemishes and imperfections.

Over the years, however, these same vegetables have taken me on a journey of discovery about the food we eat. I now look at them in a completely new light. I love the fact that my food comes with the soil still attached to it. This reminds me that my food comes not from a plastic bag but from the ground. Scrubbing the soil off my carrots gives me contact with the earth that produced it and reminds me of the labour that went into growing it (though I confess I don't particularly enjoy finding slugs in my vegetable drawer!).

I now love the fact that the vegetables come in seasons. Again, it brings me back into contact with nature, away from the bright lights and plastic bags of the supermarkets. It teaches me that things have their seasons – a very biblical idea – and helps me to appreciate the rhythm that is in life (Psalm 1:3; Ecclesiastes 3:1–8). There is no doubt, too, that many vegetables grown and harvested in season taste far better than the vegetables I used to buy, and so waiting brings a greater appreciation for them.

I have also grown to love my vegetables coming in all different shapes and sizes with their lumps and bumps. I now positively dislike having to buy vegetables in the supermarket: the rows of perfectly shaped and identically sized produce depress me. How did they get like that anyway?

One answer is that anything that does not meet the industry or supermarket standards regarding length, size, lack of blemishes and so on is thrown away. The other answer is that vegetables and fruits are produced like that through the use of chemicals: insecticides, herbicides and pesticides. Over 17,800 tonnes of pesticides were applied to UK crops in 2015 and, altogether, 300 different pesticides are permitted for use in non-organic farming. (This contrasts with only twenty pesticides allowed under organic farming standards, derived from natural ingredients and only used in very restricted circumstances.) For example, an average of thirty-three pesticides are used on UK orchard crops (apples, pears, plums and cherries), which are sprayed seventeen times. Many of these pesticides are systemic, which means they permeate into the flesh of the fruit, and so cannot be removed through peeling or washing. According to Pesticide Action Network UK, approximately 60% of British non-organic fruit and vegetables contains pesticides. Many of these contain residues of multiple pesticides. If all farming were organic, the amount of pesticides used would decrease by 98%.

Bringing up children has turned many people, including me, towards organic food.[1] Although overall organic food accounts for only 1.5% of total food and drink sales in the UK, and 4% of food and drink sales in the US, since writing this book I have seen it go from fringe and somewhat weird to mainstream. In both the UK and the US, organic food and drink sales are growing by over 6% each year, faster than non-organic sales, and 2017 saw UK home delivery of organic produce (i.e. from box schemes) grow by 10.5%.

The damage being done to the environment and to biodiversity is only too evident when you look at the difference in wildlife on organic and intensive farms. Research has found that plant, animal and insect life is more abundant on organic farms, which are home to 30% more species. Some endangered species on farmland were found only on organic farms. There were 44% more birds in fields outside the breeding season, and again endangered birds such as the song thrush were significantly more numerous on organic farms. In particular, there were more than twice as many breeding skylarks.

Intensive farming has been happening for only the past seventy years – the post-war period when, understandably, rationing caused by a loss of food imports led the government to produce a new food policy that would encourage maximum production. The consumer's constant desire for cheap food has encouraged this to continue so that since the 1950s we have seen a huge increase in production, while prices have fallen. The way that our world has developed since then has allowed us to import whatever we want, whenever we want. This has benefited us with cheap food all year round and an endless variety of products – and a proliferation of TV shows and competitions to match!

We are now beginning to realize, however, that cheap food is coming at a heavy cost. Apart from the effects of intensive farming on the environment and on biodiversity, there is also the effect of the transport and packaging involved. It is thought that 75% of the cost of food is in its processing, packaging and distribution. We often hear now about the issue of 'food miles', and it is a sobering fact that food accounts for 23% of freight moved by UK heavy-goods vehicles, more than any other commodity.

Then there are the implications for our health: many of us will hardly need reminding of salmonella, BSE, foot-and-mouth disease and bird flu. Moving away from the negative, though, there are thought to be positive benefits in eating organic foods. Research carried out since the first edition of this book now shows that no other food has higher amounts of beneficial minerals, essential amino acids and vitamins than organic food. For example, according to research conducted by European scientists, organic milk has nearly 56% more essential fatty acid omega-3 than its non-organic equivalent, and research in the *British Journal of Nutrition* found increased concentrations of anti-oxidants and other beneficial compounds in organic food.

The welfare of farmed animals is also extremely important. Thanks to factory farming, the meat that was most expensive when my parents were children (chicken) and the fish that was most expensive when I was a child (salmon) are now among the cheapest that can be bought. When you look at the conditions in which both are produced, however, you understand why. Instead of describing the life of a battery chicken, let me quote the wonderful chef, Hugh Fearnley-Whittingstall, who says that anyone who buys such meat is 'either an idiot or a heartless bastard'. The same conditions apply to the salmon that is now available, so I try not to eat salmon unless it is from an organic farm or MSC-certified (see further, 'K is for Kippers').

These issues have been publicized much more since I first wrote this book. In 2008 British chefs Hugh Fearnley-Whittingstall and Jamie Oliver were at the forefront of a highly publicized campaign to stop consumers buying intensively farmed chickens. At the time the campaign seemed to be working, as demand for higher-welfare chicken rocketed. However, all these years on, it is noticeable that we haven't sustained this move, and so supermarkets are now stocking less higher-welfare meat and more factory farmed (Waitrose being a positive exception in this regard). Sadly, little has changed to ensure good welfare standards for chickens and other animals. My own little adventures in keeping laying hens and rearing pigs and chickens for meat have only served to heighten my appreciation for these issues (and shown me that there really is a huge difference in the quality of the meat produced). It is crucial that, as Christians, we only use our money to support those who look after the animals that we will eat. After all, as Proverbs in the Old Testament wisdom literature says, 'The righteous care for the needs of their animals' (12:10).

As touched on in the previous chapter, we have become increasingly aware of the global consequences of our high meat and dairy consumption. Back in 2006 the UN's Food and Agricultural Organization brought out a ground-breaking report called *Livestock's Long Shadow*, which claimed that meat and dairy production contributes more to climate change than the entire global transport sector combined. There has been a lot of dispute about the exact figures and particularly the comparison with transport, but the key points remain: the livestock industry is 'one of the top two or three most significant contributors to the most serious environmental problems, at every scale from local to global', contributing to land degradation, climate change, air pollution, water shortage and water pollution, and a loss of biodiversity. Contributing to this is the huge growth in global meat consumption, especially by the wealthier developing countries such as India, China and Brazil. This places an extra responsibility on those of us who are used to a high meat and dairy diet, to reduce it significantly (if not cut it out altogether) in order to give others their fair share of what is sustainable.

One massive change that has occurred in recent years in the UK is the growing move towards plant-based diets and the image change that has taken place along with it. As a family, we have been gradually moving that way for years, beginning with starting the pig cooperative out of a desire to ensure our meat came from animals that were well looked after, then questioning the pig feed. (Where was it grown? Could we guarantee it was organic? Would the land used to grow the feed be used better to grow crops for people to eat? Etc.) And we took a big jump forward some years back when Jemba asked if we could do a meat-free Lent together, which got us entirely off meat for six weeks and experimenting with different recipes and new vegetables. As I mentioned earlier, we came out of the pig cooperative when I realized my freezer was full of meat we weren't eating (I've now turned off my chest freezer and just have a small one – more energy savings), and now we are almost entirely plant-based, though one or two of us will eat meat if in a situation where it can't be avoided or we can guarantee it has been well reared. This is often called 'flexitarian' – an approach that many people are now taking.

Alongside all this is an issue of power. This is not so much about the farmers: the majority care strongly for their animals and for their land, including those who are non-organic.[2] And, as has been well documented, farming is in a crisis. Between 2013 and 2015 nearly one in ten dairy farms across England and Wales closed down. And the situation in India is worse. In fact, if you type 'Indian farmers' into your search engine, the first thing that comes up is 'suicide': nearly 60,000 farmers and farm workers have committed suicide over the past thirty years.

The problem lies with those who control what happens in farming: the biotechnology companies that produce the pesticides and the GM seeds; the big food manufacturers that can influence what kind of food is grown and consumed; and the supermarkets that control distribution and dictate prices and uniformity of produce. Eighty per cent of money spent on food is spent at the supermarkets (with a big growth in online shopping), 19% of money spent on food and drink in the UK is spent at Tesco, and it is now the case that one in every eight pounds in the British economy is spent at Tesco, Aldi or Lidl. Pivotal to these is the government, which should be better involved in issues of food labelling, safety standards and supporting good farming practices.

As poet and environmental activist Wendell Berry says, how and what we eat is a political issue – an issue of freedom:

> There is a politics of food that, like any politics, involves our freedom. We still (sometimes) remember that we cannot be free if our minds and voices are controlled by someone else. But we have neglected to understand that we cannot be free

if our food and our sources are controlled by someone else. The condition of the passive consumer of food is not a democratic condition. One reason to eat responsibly is to eat free.[3]

Our attitude to food is influenced by other aspects of our lives. The chapter 'S is for Simplicity' shows how our use of time reflects our values and affects many areas of our lives. This is no less true with regard to food. Biblically, food is a part of the gift relationship that God established with humanity in the Garden of Eden. We see there the goodness of food as a gift from God to sustain us. This is reflected in the way we use food as a central part of our relationship building. Our demand for convenience, as seen already in 'D is for Driving', threatens to erode the relational aspect of food, as well as contributing to the mounting problem of food waste (see action point below).

There is thus a spiritual side to food. See how often the Bible links food and eating with central biblical concepts (communion, the water of life, fasting, 'taste and see that the LORD is good', the eschatological banquet and so on). Author and Christian environmentalist Michael Schut views food as a sacrament, and talks of 'the spirituality embodied in our personal and cultural relationship to food'.[4] I see the food I eat and the way I produce it as one of the ways in which I worship God; eating and producing in a manner that respects what he has created, both human and non-human. As Christians we must do no less.

### Action points

- Buy seasonal, local, organic food, and reduce your reliance on supermarkets (but see 'Q is for Questions' for a more detailed discussion). Farm shops, delivery boxes and farmers' markets are great ways to do this. (The Soil Association provides information on these.) Get together with friends to form a food cooperative, enabling you to buy organic and Fairtrade food at wholesale prices (see e.g. Infinity Foods, <www. infinityfoodswholesale.coop>). If you have to choose, go local rather than organic, but try to do both! Green Christian, <https://greenchristian.org.uk> has devised a useful mnemonic – just follow the LOAF principle: Local, Organic, Animal friendly and Fairly traded.

- Grow (and rear!) your own food. Whether you have an allotment or just a windowsill, you can grow some of your own things, making the connection between your food and the land. You will know exactly what has gone into it, and the food miles will be zero.

- Question your supermarket constantly (contact Friends of the Earth's 'What to Eat' food campaign, and see 'B is for Bananas' for more on Fairtrade). Let them know what you would like their policies to be. ('L is for Letters' looks further at this.) If you use different supermarkets, compare their answers.

- Shop wisely and only buy what you will eat. A third of food is currently thrown away by wealthy consumers, contributing to climate change which is increasing world poverty and hunger. (For more on how to reduce food waste, see Tearfund's Renew Our Food campaign and <www.wrap.org.uk>.)

## Notes

1. I am concentrating on vegetables and fruit here, but the same can, of course, also be said of meat, with the little-known

dangers of eating animals that have regularly been given antibiotics and are themselves eating feeds that contain pesticides.

2. A positive development in farming is a move towards 'integrated farm management', a system that includes the use of traditional techniques along with modern pesticides and aims to minimize environmental impact. The view is that pesticides contribute importantly to our health and quality of life by, for example, enabling crops to be produced more efficiently, reducing the contamination of food by toxic fungi, and controlling insects that spread human diseases. Recognizing potential dangers, however, their approach is that one should 'use as much pesticide as is necessary to do the job, but as little as possible'. For more details, contact the Crop Protection Association UK at <www.cropprotection.org.uk> and the British Crop Protection Council at <www.bcpc.org>. Food produced under this system bears the LEAF marque (Linking Environment and Farming: see <www.leafmarque.com>).

3. Wendell Berry, 'The Pleasures of Eating', in Michael Schut (ed.), *Simpler Living, Compassionate Life: A Christian Perspective* (Earth Ministry, 1999), p. 106.

4. Michael Schut, 'Food as Sacrament', in *Earth Letter* (November 2001), p. 11.

# G IS FOR GLOBALIZATION

'Let's see how many countries we represent today,' I said to my seminar group. 'Have a look at the clothes you're wearing, the bag you're carrying, your phone . . . and see where they all come from.' As people called out, it soon became clear we were wearing and using things from all around the world: jeans from Morocco, a pen from Malaysia, an apple from New Zealand, a bag from Bali, a diary from China . . .

In 'A is for Activists' we looked at what it means to be a people who want to spend themselves on behalf of the hungry and satisfy the needs of the oppressed (Isaiah 58:10). If we are to work effectively in our world, we need to understand the context in which our world is set.

This is where 'globalization' comes in. The World Bank, WTO and IMF define it as 'the growing economic interdependence of countries worldwide through increasing volume and variety of cross-border transactions in goods and services, freer international capital flows, and more rapid and widespread diffusion of technology'. The Department for International Development (DFID) says it is simply 'the process by which the world is becoming more and more connected and interdependent'. The seminar answers proved the point. In particular, since the events of 9/11, with war and instability in the Middle East and the threat of terrorism, we are realizing how interlinked our world is.

Globalization is bound up with the theory of free-trade market capitalism (that is, trade liberalization, privatization and financial market deregulation). It carries with it the view that free trade between nations, with no protective barriers, is the most effective way of increasing global wealth and of lifting poorer countries out of poverty. It is certainly true that market capitalism has led to increasing global wealth, as the proportion of GDP traded internationally has risen from 24% in 1960 to 56% at the time of writing. This more-than-doubling increase in world trade is phenomenal, and reflects a world very different from that of 1960, one in which transport and communication cost less, there are strong trade agreements (especially among developing countries), and more companies have now outsourced parts of their business to lower-cost economies. It is a world in which China is now the world's leading exporter, and the rise of the internet has made it easier to purchase international goods and services.

As we saw earlier, this incredible rise in global wealth *has* resulted in a concomitant fall in poverty, with fewer people going to bed hungry every night, more people living longer, and more children being educated.[1] The Growth Lab's work at Harvard's Center for International Development has shown that economic growth is the single most important factor in increasing living standards and reducing poverty. The link is so clear that economic growth is one of the Sustainable Development Goals (#8), which aims for 7% annual GDP growth in 'Less-developed Countries' between 2011 and 2020. It might not be a surprise, then, to learn that world economic growth is coming not from the richest, developed countries, but from the emerging markets (chiefly China and India). Between 2009 and 2016, developed countries experienced 1% average annual real GDP growth, compared to 4.9% for developing countries.

Globalization has therefore brought many benefits. Alongside the fall in poverty, perhaps the biggest is that we live in an increasingly peaceful world (and that the two are linked, I hope, is obvious). This may sound an odd thing to say when our news feeds are filled with images of conflict from places such as Syria, South Sudan and Mexico, and I don't want to be misunderstood: there are some terrible wars taking place (ten at the time of writing), and the impact of these on poverty and environmental destruction is, again I hope, obvious. Conflict is one of the biggest factors in poverty today, and why Tearfund has chosen conflict as one of its key areas of work. And yet, despite these wars and the ubiquitous 'war on terror', our world is actually at its most peaceful – probably in its most peaceful period in history. In an increasingly interlinked world, it doesn't pay to be at war. However, this peace is extremely fragile, and as followers of the Prince of Peace, we must keep praying for it, and standing against policies and rhetoric that threaten to undermine it rather than build it up.

There are two particular issues that need facing in the context of globalization. The first is the recognition that despite the fall in poverty, there is rising wealth inequality between the world's richest and poorest people. Overall, the gap between the top and bottom fifths of the world's people jumped from 30:1 in 1960 to 74:1 in 1997. According to Oxfam, the world's richest forty-two people own as much wealth as the 3.7 billion poorest people, making up half of the world's population. Oxfam's research also found that 82% of all wealth generated in 2017 went to the world's richest 1%. A 2017 Credit Suisse report backed this up, showing that the globe's richest 1% own half the world's wealth, up from 46% in 2000. The so-called Paradise Papers scandal in 2017 revealed how politicians, high-end wealthy individuals and multi-nationals limit the tax they pay ('tax dodging') by using offshore finance structures. This corrupt system, alongside the corruption at the heart of some national governments, contributes to the extreme wealth inequality we are seeing today, as does the problem of heads of corporations paying themselves too much and their workers too little. There are huge issues here around the erosion of workers' rights, the excessive influence of big business over government policy-making, and the relentless corporate drive to minimize costs in order to maximize returns to shareholders.[2]

The second issue is the recognition that globalization may have led to a rise in global wealth, but that has resulted in the extreme environmental issues we are now facing. Economic development has not happened sustainably. One of the scariest passages in Hans Rosling's helpful book, *Factfulness: Ten Reasons We're Wrong about the World – and Why Things Are Better than You Think*, is his statement: 'There are 5 billion potential consumers out there, improving their lives in the middle, and wanting to consume shampoo, motorcycles, menstrual pads, and smartphones.'[3] As we will see in 'N is for Needs', consumerism goes hand in hand with global-ization, and we haven't worked out how to consume in a way that doesn't push us over our planetary boundaries. That is the key challenge facing our world today, and the reason why Tearfund bases much of what it does on its Restorative Economy work, which calls for an economy that

keeps inequality within reasonable limits and enables everyone to meet their basic needs within a flourishing natural
world.[4]

One thing is clear: for the foreseeable future, globalization
is here to stay. We live in a globalized economy, and opting
out is not an option. So the key question is: what kind
of globalization do we want? And the answer must be a
globalization that works for people in poverty, is pro social
justice and respects the Earth's limits.

So how do we respond? In many ways, this whole book is
a response to globalization, and many action suggestions in
other chapters relate here too. It is crucial that we keep
supporting ethical business practices and standards, as well as
opposing illegal and/or immoral business abuses. When we
engage with globalization through our purchasing practices
(and remember, that includes more intangible things such as
where we get our energy from too), let's choose to purchase
from the most ethical companies with the best environmental
and labour practices.

Of course, from a Christian perspective, it is good to note
that the Bible too has a strong global vision. Whether it is
the foundational call of Abram (Genesis 12:3), the words
of the prophets (e.g. Isaiah 49:6), the universality of Jesus'
message (e.g. Matthew 8:11) or the inclusivity of Paul looking
ahead to the judgment seat (Romans 14:11), we see that God's
salvation plans for humanity were not restricted to one group
of people, but were for all nations, united together before the
God who made them.

Revelation brings the vision in all its glory to a climax.
Before the throne of God stands 'a great multitude that
no one could count, from every nation, tribe, people and
language' (7:9). At the heart of this scene is Jesus, the Lamb;
the biblical vision finds its centre and fulfilment in him.

The universality of the Bible goes right against global-ization's treatment of culture. One of the criticisms levelled at globalization is that it has destroyed local cultures while promoting US culture: the 'McDonaldization' of the world. And, of course, this has contributed to anti-Western views in conservative Middle Eastern countries, fuelling the growth of terrorism. As the Bible unfolds, however, it is clear that every culture is acceptable and valid as a vehicle for God's revelation. This both relativizes and gives value to individual cultures in a way that globalization does not, and hence leads the way to a peaceful interculturality as opposed to ethnic conflict.

While globalization itself might be neutral, the biblical vision demonstrates that Christians have a global dream far more fulfilling than that offered by globalization. As Alex Araujo says, 'Globalization is the current strategy that a secular and lost humanity has developed to cope with an existence devoid of faith and hope in God.'[5]

Author Tom Sine is particularly clear on the need to show the Christian hope that can be brought to a world caught in the clutches of globalization. He claims, 'The only way we can begin to contend with the seductions of McWorld is to offer a more compelling dream than the Western Dream.'[6] This dream is of a renewed, transformed heaven and earth, 'in which justice comes for the poor, the instruments of warfare are transformed into the instruments of peace and festive banqueting and celebration will welcome us home'.[7] As we continue living in this globalized world, let us make sure that it is this basic vision that drives our faith and our churches.

### Action points

- Look at the food you buy, the clothes you wear, the equipment you use. Where are they from? Develop an awareness of the interconnectedness of your life with other people and environments all over the world, and the impact that your consumer choices have on others.

- Get involved in campaigns that are working for a fairer global economic system and opposing unfair trade deals, such as Global Justice Now, <www.globaljustice. org.uk>.
- Subscribe to *Ethical Consumer* magazine.

### Notes

1. For more on this, see Hans Rosling, *Factfulness: Ten Reasons We're Wrong about the World – and Why Things Are Better than You Think* (Sceptre, 2018).
2. Naomi Klein's writings are very helpful to read in this regard.
3. Rosling, *Factfulness*, p. 32.
4. See Tearfund, *The Restorative Economy: Completing Our Unfinished Millennium Jubilee*. And see similarly Kate Raworth's Doughnut Economics model and the thinking about the Circular Economy, coming from the Ellen MacArthur Foundation, <www.ellenmacarthurfoundation.org>.
5. A. Araujo, 'Globalization and World Evangelism', in William D. Taylor (ed.), *Global Missiology* (Baker, 2001), p. 60.
6. Tom W. Sine, Jr, 'Globalization, Creation of Global Culture Consumption and the Impact on the Church and Its Mission' (2004) (see <www.globalmissiology.org>).
7. Tom W. Sine, Jr, 'Globalization'.

# H IS FOR HABITATS

When Jemba was eight years old, she announced she would no longer eat or use products made with palm oil. Thanks to a love of orangutans and Michael Morpurgo's *Running Wild*, she discovered that huge swathes of the Malaysian and Indonesian tropical rainforests had been burnt down to provide land for palm oil plantations, seriously impacting orangutans. Between 1999 and 2015, the population of orangutans in Borneo more than halved, lost along with their forest homes. For an eight-year-old, avoiding palm oil was a big sacrifice, as it pretty much meant no biscuits, no sweets and nothing processed. (It was a big sacrifice for me too, as I was the one who had to make it work for her! Start looking on the backs of packaging and you'll be amazed how much palm oil there is.) I have been very impressed with Jemba's dedication as she has stuck resolutely with her decision for many years now.

The example of palm oil and orangutans is not unique. There has been a staggering 89% decline in species in South and Central America, and an 83% decline in global freshwater species since 1970. I want to ask you to stop at this point and let that sink in. May we not allow these to become cold statistics that don't impact us!

A significant driver for this is habitat loss. Sometimes this is as extreme as cutting down habitats and replacing them with spaces that can't support the existing species. Other times it's more subtle: fragmenting a habitat by building a road through a woodland so that animals can't reach their mates, or polluting a habitat with an invasive species or harmful chemicals.

This is a crisis.

But maybe it doesn't feel quite like one. Perhaps it feels as if it's happening far away, or if we live in an urban area, we are not aware enough of wildlife to notice our spaces becoming increasingly sterile.

I remember watching wildlife presenter Chris Packham walking through a new housing estate, commenting that it was absolutely silent. There were no birds, no bees, no butterflies . . . it was a human-made desert that allowed no space for other creatures to thrive.

God loves diversity. In 'C is for Creation' we saw that God created this world and he loves it – and he created an earth that was teeming with life. It is this life together, in all its fullness, that he calls 'very good'. God delights in us living within the diverse world he has made. The destruction of the places and creatures that call those places home must cause him immense sorrow.

So how can we begin to help? The best place to start is on our own doorstep. Studies show that if you have a personal experience of nature, you are much more likely to want to take care of it. This is particularly so for children, who are more likely to become passionate about conservation if they have had lots of contact with the wider natural world.

Are there spaces near you where you can bring wildlife back in?

As agricultural areas become more hostile to animals and insects, many species rely on gardens, hedges and rooftops for homes. However, trends for plastic lawns, paving for car parking and garden pesticides mean that these spaces are no longer liveable habitats. Previously common species of butterflies, bees and garden birds are in rapid decline. Worryingly, in Germany insect populations have declined by 76% in the past twenty-seven years. There are similar trends in the rest of the world. Not only should they exist in their own right, but we need these species to survive. Without insects, we cannot grow the plants we need to survive.

So grow bee-friendly blooms in your garden (the bees absolutely love our weigela bush), and place some upturned plant pots to create shelter for them and other insects. Plants such as nettles and ivy are nesting sites for butterflies, so only trim hedges in winter, when their eggs won't be there. You could even create a bee hotel made of bamboo canes or a block of wood with drilled holes for resting bees. We have a pile of leaves on the lawn from a hedge we trimmed that we hadn't tidied away, and I noticed the other day that there were frogs in it from our pond. That pile of leaves will have to stay!

You could research declining local species in your area to see if there are practical ways you can support them in creating a home. For example, house martins were previously a common garden bird in the UK, but their numbers have rapidly declined. These tiny birds make nests out of mud, but there is less mud to be found, with drier weather from climate change and new house designs that don't provide the nesting spaces of the older houses. One simple tip from the Royal

Society for the Protection of Birds (RSPB) is to make damp mud in containers or flower beds that they can use: 'creating just a small patch of mud at the side of your garden could make a real difference to a pair of house martins.'[1]

If you want to think bigger than your own garden, or you do not have one, you can also see if there are local areas that can become wildlife habitats. The American National Wildlife Federation (NWF) has a helpful guide for turning yards, balcony container gardens, schoolyards, work landscapes or roadside green spaces into wildlife havens.

As we will see later in 'O is for Organic', we must also change what gardening products we use and stop using pesticides. The problem of pesticides on habitats is much bigger than domestic use, but by their very nature, pesticides harm animals and insects, so let's avoid using them in our gardens. A BBC *Gardeners' World* survey showed that two-thirds of people were taking measures such as avoiding using slug pellets to look after hedgehogs. My mother-in-law and I are in a constant fight together to stop slugs eating our vegetables. We have tried all sorts of things – eggshells, coffee grinds, beer and even sheep wool – with varying degrees of success!

As citizens, we can lobby our town and city planners to include natural spaces in urban areas. The benefits of this are felt by more than just the local wildlife. Natural spaces improve quality of life for humans too, and have been shown to improve the economic success of an area.

However, habitat loss isn't simply about the animals and plants on our doorsteps. Our actions also affect habitats much further afield.

Let's go back to palm oil. Global palm oil has more than doubled since the 1980s. Part of the attraction of palm oil as a crop is that it is multi-purpose and high-yielding, producing significantly more oil per tonne than other vegetable oils, and it can be separated to make lots of different products. You will find it in a range of products as varied as ice cream, lipstick and biofuel. Unlike other oils, however, it grows only in tropical regions. Since the 1980s, huge tracts of tropical forest in Asia and in Africa have been cleared for palm plantations, destroying the habitats of rare and endangered species. I remember being in Singapore about twenty years ago, and for the whole time I was there I didn't see the sun once because of the haze from the Indonesian forest fires. It was shocking. Avoiding palm oil is certainly a good step, as is looking out for products that use certified sustainable palm oil, and we can also contact companies to ask them to do the same.

But palm oil is not the only crop causing habitat destruction. One of the biggest drivers of habitat loss is agriculture: plants and animals farmed to create food, fuel or clothing for humans and their pets. In fact, 96% of mammals on Earth are livestock and humans, and only 4% are wild: a significant shift in the past fifty years. And so animal farming is also a big contributor to habitat loss in vulnerable habitats, due to land clearing to convert rainforests and savannas into large farms that produce single crops, such as soy and maize to feed animals. Without the biodiversity of the rainforest, the soil in this land quickly becomes poor and needs artificial fertilizers to grow the crops. Not only does this remove habitats for the animals living in the plants; it also affects the local water sources. These fertilizers can run off into local rivers and lakes, triggering harmful algal blooms, where the fertilizers feed algae in the water and cause too much to grow. These blooms cut off oxygen to other animals and plants, and cause huge dead spots. The land can degrade so much that it can no longer be used for farming, so more virgin rainforest then needs to be destroyed.

As we have seen already, cutting down the amount of meat we consume makes a real difference. This does not mean that everyone needs to become a vegan. Even if we just reduced our meat intake to the recommended nutritional amounts, we would make a difference. For example, according to the WWF's Livewell report, people in the UK eat on average 64–88 g of protein per day, with 37% of this being meat protein. If everyone reduced their protein consumption to the recommended UK nutritional guidelines of 45–55 g, we would need 13% less agricultural land. And it's helpful to remember that some meats are more resource-intensive than others: beef, for example, requires significantly more grain than chicken or pork.

Alongside thinking about the things we buy, we can financially support organizations working to conserve habitats and, through them, get involved in shaping the policies of governments, institutions and corporations on these issues. There are so many good organizations here: both WWF (the World Wildlife Fund) and A Rocha are doing excellent work that requires us to get involved, both financially and with our voices.

It can sometimes feel a bit gloomy and overwhelming to think about the problems of habitat loss. The best remedy is to take time to enjoy wildlife wherever we are, in order to remind us that it is worth protecting.

**Action points**

- Take steps to make your garden a welcoming place for wildlife.
- Try to avoid products with palm oil, or only buy products made with sustainable palm oil.
- Reduce the amount of meat and dairy you eat.

- Find an organization working to protect habitats that you can support. Alongside WWF and A Rocha, the Zoological Society of London's website is also a good place to look.

**Note**

1. RSPB, 'Have you seen a house martin?' (see <www.rspb.org.uk>).

## I IS FOR INVESTMENTS

Most of us will have savings and investments in one form or another. That might mean just a current account, or we may have invested in the stock market. We may have ISAs, National Savings or bonds. The majority of us will, at some point, have a mortgage and a pension. Do we ever ask ourselves what that money is being used for – where exactly has our bank or pension provider put the money we're giving them?

YMCA Downslink Group is a registered charity working in the south of the UK to provide a variety of services and projects to local communities. Their focus is helping young people who exist on the margins of society to access opportunities and ultimately feel as if they can thrive in adult life. Last year they reached over 16,000 young people through supported housing, learning and employability projects, counselling services and more.

When it is completed, Sandford Hydro will be the largest hydro-electric plant on the Thames, using the power of the river to generate approximately 1.6 GWh of clean electricity each year – enough to power around 500 households, nearly the full Sandford village. It is a community enterprise, run by locals, and specially designed to have minimum impact on wildlife and the ecosystem.

Bina Artha is a micro-finance institution that provides sanitation loans for in-house toilets in Indonesia – a country where 40% of the 100 million population can't afford proper sanitation. Bina Artha provides funding to help people in this situation, and also helps borrowers set up businesses in order to pay back loans and ultimately further improve their long-term living conditions.

All these charities and businesses have recently received loans to help them improve their work, from banks that operate on an ethical basis. Perhaps my money has played a part in the work they do? I hope so.

By contrast, in another part of the world a corporation's activities are destroying the livelihoods of the indigenous people and polluting the environment, in order to increase shareholder profits. Perhaps my money has allowed this to happen? I hope not.

Throughout this book we are looking at how we can use our lives to help the world. The good news is that what we do with our money can play a significant part. For those of us who are financially wealthy (on a global level), actively seeking to do good with our money isn't just a responsibility; it's a definite blessing!

In 'M' we shall look at the wider subject of money.[1] The principle guiding this chapter, though, is that the question of money is not only about how much we give but also about what we do with what we keep.

The first questions to ask are: should a Christian have investments in the first place? And, if so, what is an appropriate level? Does saving anything demonstrate a lack of faith in God's provision, or does *not* saving demonstrate a lack of prudence and good stewardship? The Bible seems to teach both (compare Proverbs 6:8; 21:20 with Matthew 6:19). Lest we answer too quickly that Jesus' teaching should always come before that of the Old Testament, we should not forget that he himself depended on the support of wealthy women, and did not demand that Nicodemus or Joseph of Arimathea give away all their money in order to be his disciples.

The Bible gives two positive reasons for saving financially: first, we save in order to fulfil our family obligations (Mark 7:9–13; 1 Timothy 5:8), and, second, we save in order not to be dependent on anyone (2 Thessalonians 3:6–12). Alongside this is the continual and overarching reminder that we must use any money or possessions we have to help the poor (e.g. Ephesians 4:28). Nowhere does the Bible say we should invest simply to gain more money in order to become more financially secure (look at the Parable of the Rich Fool in Luke 12:13–21).

This does, of course, still leave room for interpretation as to what it means. How far does our family extend? How much should we leave our children? How much do we need in order to prevent dependence? In this, as with so much, the Bible's teaching gives us parameters, but not a single, universally applicable norm. The appropriate attitude to wealth would seem to depend on the Christian's situation and calling (for instance, to the mission field, to a dependent family, to singleness).

What we need to remember at all times is our natural inclination to justify saving the most we can. We must always guard ourselves against the desire to accumulate as much as possible in order to make ourselves as secure as possible.

Beyond this, though, a further question to ask is *how* should we save: what forms should our investments take? Surprisingly perhaps, the Bible provides a fair amount of guidance on this matter. Looking after our money, as well as the rest of creation, is a key principle: taking personal responsibility ourselves, not just letting others control our finances for us, and also ensuring that any business activity we are involved in promotes the welfare of creation and doesn't contribute to its destruction. Relationships are always central and placed above the accumulation of wealth. Accountability and openness are important, therefore, so that we know to what purposes our savings are being put. The Bible places a ban on interest (though Protestant Christianity has allowed a distinction between usury – charging high interest rates – and lending money at low interest rates). Finally, the Bible is clear that no money should be acquired at the expense of someone else, or through dishonesty.

If these principles are followed, it will soon be apparent how starkly they stand in opposition to the accepted forms of investment that the majority of us as Christians follow today. For example, generally our shares are held in large companies where there is no local accountability or relational basis. Some banks likewise give depositors no control over the use of their finances, or over the way the bank conducts its relationships with borrowers.

Perhaps most important for the purposes of this book is the fact that so much conventional saving today is in companies that exploit their customers, their workers and the created world. As Christians, we have a responsibility to see where our money is going, and to ensure it is not being used to the detriment of others or the environment.

Our money might be invested in a wide variety of ways (some of which might not cause you a problem personally).

However, it might be used for the production and sale of military hardware or fossil fuels, involved in pornography, the fur trade or tobacco production. It could be used by an oppressive regime that tramples on human rights, or it could be involved in intensive farming, environmentally destructive mining, the illegal felling of tropical hardwoods or water pollution. Our money could be used for currency speculation, which can damage a nation's economy, or it might even be used to service a poorer country's debt. We need to be aware of the power of our money and, where possible, ensure it is being used in ethical ways.

Thankfully, we *can* do something, and we *can* control what happens to our money if we are prepared to expend some time and thought. Ethical investments are on the rise and increasingly easy to come by for all investment purposes, including mortgages and pensions, bonds and savings accounts. In fact, there has been a big growth in ethical lending – as well as investment – in both the UK and US. In the UK, ethical lending increased by 45% in 2015, creating 10,000 new businesses and 25,000 jobs, and in the US, ethical investment grew by 33% between 2014 and 2017, accounting for 20% of investments under professional management. On a personal level, there are now more than 150 ethical investment funds in the UK to choose from, as well as ethical bonds and savings, and in the US there are over 180 socially responsible investment funds (SRIs).

There has also been a huge growth in microfinance: 9% p.a., for people who have no access to loans from a financial institution. It's amazing to think that, through this, 130 million people, mainly rural women living in developing countries, have now received microfinance. We can be a part of this by choosing to put our money with banks or organizations that work in this area, such as Shared Interest, <www.shared-interest.com/gb>.

The term 'ethical investments' covers a broad spectrum, and different approaches are used. Some options work 'negatively' (by not investing in particular concerns, such as the arms trade, fossil fuel companies or tobacco), whereas other options work 'positively' (investing only in companies that are specifically working for social or environmental enhancement). A third option is what's known as the 'best-of-sector' approach. This allows investment in *every* sector, but only on the basis of selecting the companies that are the most ethical/environmentally conscious within those sectors, or making significant progress. A key to this approach is the idea of engagement: that by being involved in the shareholdings of a company, influence can be brought to bear to bring about change. So, for example, if a fossil fuel company is deemed to be making progress towards the Paris climate commitments, then this approach would allow investment in that company.[2] It is therefore really important that we do our own thinking around what sort of approach we want, and go into any investment option with our eyes open and aware of the criteria being used. One key thing to look for is openness and transparency in how an investment option works. For example, Triodos Bank produces a regular newsletter for its investors, giving details of the different businesses and projects to which it is lending.

Some of us may own substantial sums of money. If that is the case, there are stockbrokers with entire ethical/environmental research departments who will sit down with a client and establish an individual ethical screen. Another option is to become a 'business angel', someone who invests money and becomes a shareholder in a small business, often giving advice and expertise too. This must be one of the best ways to invest any extra money we might have: there is a good balance of risk and return. Close relationships are often fostered, helping us know exactly where our money is going, thus enhancing our role as stewards. Cred Jewellery was enabled to succeed because of two such 'business angels', and they were key in therefore enabling Fairtrade gold to become a reality.

Some of us might not have large amounts of money to invest, but would still like to be active in pushing companies to change. ShareAction is a useful group to look at – they encourage individuals to buy single shares of large companies, which then entitles them to attend AGMs and lobby for improvements in environmental / ethical practices. They also advise on responsible pensions.

However much money we have, as well as thinking through where our own personal finances are invested, we can all encourage the companies or organizations we work for, and the churches we worship in, to invest more ethically. I have played my part in working to see that happen in one of the organizations I have been involved with. It takes time and effort and a willingness to listen to different viewpoints. But it is vital that we do this. Alongside this is the growing divestment movement that is seeing churches, universities and other institutions withdraw their money from fossil fuel companies and look to reinvest that money into companies working more fully for the common good of both people and planet.

However we choose to play it, the key is that whenever we put some money into an account, invest in an ISA, apply for a mortgage and so on, we have a direct opportunity to use our money to do some good in our world. And that can only be an exciting thing.

## Action points

- Look at where your money is invested. Is it being used for good or for harm?
- Take time to look into the different ethical options available. *Ethical Consumer* magazine has a regular financial section offering useful information.
- Identify an area of your financial investment that can be improved ethically. Make the necessary changes to your arrangements, and then inform your bank, mortgage lender or pension scheme manager of your reasons for the changes, and encourage them to invest ethically. When you have done this, identify a second area to change, and so on.
- Ask your church to look at how its money is invested, either through its central investment group or as an individual congregation. See Operation Noah's Bright Now campaign, <http://operationnoah.org/articles/bright-now-towards-fossil-free-churches>, for more information around divestment. If your denomination holds significant investments, then partnering with the Transition Pathway Initiative is a good option.

## Notes

1. And see also the fuller discussion in 'In Plenty or in Want: How to Think about Wealth', in Ruth Valerio, *Just Living: Faith and Community in an Age of Consumerism* (Hodder & Stoughton, 2016), ch. 5.
2. This third approach is taken by the National Investing Bodies of the Church of England, which use something called the Transition Pathway Initiative (TPI). This ground-breaking tool maps where companies are on the road to a low-carbon

economy, and so helps investors determine where to invest their monies. The TPI is seeing significant shifts in companies as a result.

# J IS FOR JOBS

Do you leap out of bed on a Monday morning, thrilled to be able to start another week's paid work, and do you come home on a Friday evening, despondent because the working week is over? Perhaps not!

Maybe though you are wondering what the subject of jobs has to do with this book. Well, being involved in God's heart for justice encompasses every area of our lives, and for many of us, work (including travel) can take up 60–70% of our waking hours. It is what the biggest portion of our lives is given over to, and the thing that, more than anything else, can inform who we are.

We are working longer hours and till later in life. The traditional age of retirement for women has been sixty, but women and men retiring in 2028 or later are likely to be at least sixty-seven. It's a similar picture in the US, with retirement age now rising from sixty-five to sixty-seven for women and men. Our working patterns are changing too, with us changing jobs and careers more often than previous generations. We now change jobs twelve times on average, and many people change career five times. Gone are the days of working for one company our whole working life, and many of us have 'portfolio' careers, with a lot less job security.

There is a difference between employment (including self-employment) and work (which can include voluntary work, that done by carers, and so on). Both contribute to the wider community; one is paid, while the other is not. There are a number of different reasons for paid employment: earning money, gaining a sense of security, tradition, enjoyment, duty, serving others, learning, prestige and status, socializing, personal growth, success, creativity, fulfilment . . . Which of these apply to you? More broadly, work has two functions: the financial and the personal. For some of us, both of these functions may be met in our jobs. For others, our job may meet the financial need primarily, and other types of reward are found in our unpaid activities.

Considering our jobs in this way helps free us from the fatalistic sense that we *have* to do whatever job we are currently doing, and opens us up to other possibilities. Why are we doing this job? Is this what we want to do? Is it what we believe God is calling us to? Did we take this career path because of cultural expectations? Is our job a result of decisions made years ago that we were unaware we were making at the time?

Some of us have got ourselves caught up in the materialistic rat race. The US journalist Ellen Goodman sums this up well: 'Normal is getting dressed in clothes that you buy for work, driving through traffic in a car that you are still paying for, in order to get to the job you need so you can pay for the clothes, car and the house that you leave empty all day in order to afford to live in it.'[1] The US financial author and broadcaster

Dave Ramsey says something similar: 'We buy things we don't need with money we don't have to impress people we don't like.'

James's story is a good example. He was a city lawyer, specializing in the investigation of international bank fraud, when he was first challenged about the claims of the Christian faith by a barrister. Three years of forensic investigation later, he accepted that what was written in the Gospels was true. But it made no difference because, as he told me, 'an intellectual faith is in reality no faith'. He was in Hong Kong on a fraud investigation and heard the testimonies of some of the ex-heroin-addict former Triad gangsters who worked with Jackie Pullinger. Their tales brought it home: if Christ has risen, he is alive and at work today. This changed everything: James left the law to work with Jackie Pullinger. Then he felt God calling him back to the UK. In time he set up a 'people's bank', working with those wanting to come off benefits and stand on their own two feet. From a large house in an upmarket part of London, he and his family moved to a bungalow in a rundown area. Their time was given to homeschooling their children and working with people in need.

James's story is not about moving from a non-Christian to a Christian option: investigating international bank fraud could be a high Christian calling. Rather, what his story illustrates is his willingness to change when God asked him to.

While this kind of lifestyle change may be an option for some, for the majority our jobs simply help us keep our heads above water. People working full-time in the UK have the longest hours of any country in the EU (an average of 42.3 hours a week), though Americans work harder at an average of 46.7 hours. Research shows that many managers have no time for other interests, and believe their work damages their health and affects their relationships with their children and partner. When you consider that a third of working UK parents say they feel burned out most of or all the time, with overwork being identified as the main source of burnout, we may begin to feel that our work–life balance is not being maintained well.

This is in direct contrast with the biblical testimony. Here work (whether paid or unpaid) is good in and of itself: something that God ordained for people to do. In Genesis 1:26–28 and 9:7 we see that God made us to work. Work is an indispensable part of what it means to be human, and even God himself is described as doing work (Genesis 2:2 and elsewhere). Work is thus an important aspect of our self-fulfilment as people, rather than something to be avoided at all costs. The search for excellence and achievement is not disparaged, but positively encouraged (as seen, for example, in the building of the tabernacle in Exodus 35).

At the same time, however, work is not the means to salvation, and there is a negative side to it, as seen in the curse of the fall. Work can be hard and painful (and certainly it can be used for wrong ends) rather than positive creativity.

Work is not the be-all and end-all: God's week of creation finished with a day to rest. Our lives should have a rhythm to them that includes time set aside to rest, and time that is specifically dedicated to worshipping God. Our vocation is not limited to work; it also includes friendship, play, love, worship and rest. Life today is sometimes characterized as 'work, eat, sleep, repeat'.

Can we find ways as Christians to break into, and out of, this sort of existence?

Because of faulty theologies that have permeated the church (particularly those that created a sacred–secular divide), we can see our workplaces as necessary for our survival, and then our churches as being where the *real* work of being a Christian takes place. Thus we may spend many hours of our day working in the supermarket, but it's the two hours we spend running the youth work that get the attention. Instead of this, we need to develop what Mark Greene describes as 'faith consciousness': a deliberate awareness of God's presence in our workplaces and an integration of our faith, our work and the rest of our lives.[2]

Is there a way of doing work differently? While we may not all be able to make the kind of changes James made above, we may still be able to find ways of working that honour God's creation and give more time for developing a closer relationship with him. What practices could you bring into your work situation? Could you build in a regular lunch break and a walk if you've got into the habit of eating your lunch in front of the computer, something I'm terrible at doing (I'd better be honest here)? Maybe you could become a Green Champion at work or use more environmentally friendly ways of commuting, or travel less, using videoconferencing for virtual meetings instead of flying, for example. Could you commit to going by train when travelling for a meeting in the UK and even in Europe (something I'm better at and enjoy doing immensely). Maybe you might decide your finances would allow you to reduce your work by one day a week, or you could build in some flexi-time and work from home sometimes.

The challenges that our workplaces present are many. We might find ourselves working in areas that perpetuate the problems we are looking at in this book, and where the rightness of our remaining is questionable. One of the most challenging aspects of Christianity is that often there are no hard-and-fast rules, but guidelines to follow and the Holy Spirit to prompt. This applies here too. God will call some of us to work within the structures that perpetuate the injustices we have looked at so far in this book. Look at Daniel. Look at Joseph. This is no easy calling: it comes accompanied by its own pressures and frustrations, working out where compromise is the right route and where it is not. God will call others of us to find work that brings us outside the structures. Look at Amos. Both positions will give us opportunities to critique and to live and speak prophetically. But, wherever we stand, we must do so knowing that this is where God has placed us.

### Action points

- Is there an attitude about your work that you need to change? Do you know that you are where God has placed you?
- What steps could you take to help your place of work become more socially and environmentally friendly?
- Find out more about Christian organizations that help people live out their faith at work, such as the London Institute of Contemporary Christianity in the UK, <www.licc.org.uk>.

### Notes

1. Ellen Goodman, cited in Janet Luhrs, *The Simple Living Guide* (Bantam Doubelday Dell, 1997).
2. Mark Greene, *Supporting Christians at Work – Without Going Insane* (Administry, 2001), p. 13, citing the '1999 Survey of Managers' Changing Experiences' from the Institute of Management.

# K IS FOR KIPPERS

One of the practical questions I am asked most when I speak on environmental care is: 'If we need to reduce the amount of meat we eat, is it okay if we just switch to fish and eat that instead?' It is a good question, and in recent years we have become increasingly aware of the fragile state of our oceans and of the creatures that live in it.

There is at least some partial good news here in that action has been, and is being, taken, and we are seeing results. In earlier editions of this book I started this chapter with my local fish'n'chip shop, which had a sign up informing its customers that all its cod came from Icelandic waters and not from the North Sea. Apparently, the owner had had so many customers telling him they didn't want to eat North Sea cod that he changed where he got his fish from. At that point North Sea cod was in danger of total collapse.

Never would we have imagined that in 2017, North Sea cod fisheries would be awarded the MSC gold standard for sustainability! This was due to a successful 'Cod Recovery Plan' that nursed cod stocks back to health. The EU introduced measures to control and reduce fishing and catch restrictions. In addition, the UK government devised catch quotas, stopping fishing when catch limits were reached, and incentivized fishing more selectively. Cod levels are now back to where they were in 1980, though recovery is still fragile. This shows what's possible when fishermen work together with fisheries managers, scientists, the wider industry and government to recover fish stocks.

Sadly, this good news story doesn't give the whole picture. According to the 2016 'State of the World's Fisheries and Aquaculture' report (SOFIA), the state of the world's marine fish stocks has not improved overall in the past forty-five years. In 1970, 90% of fish stocks were at biologically sustainable levels, but by 2013 this had dropped to 69%.

The modern practice of bottom trawling (whereby nets, often weighted, and sometimes with metal beams or hydraulic dredges, are dragged across the sea floor to catch prawns and bottom-dwelling fish) is one of the main reasons for the decline of fish stocks. Bottom trawling destroys the thick natural carpet of plants and animals that live on the sea floor, necessary for the survival of the fry of fish such as cod, and can damage or destroy species such as corals and sponges that take years to recolonize. Both midwater and bottom trawling are hugely wasteful, producing high levels of bycatch, or unwanted fish, that are then tossed back overboard, often dead or dying. According to recent research, 10% of world catch from industrial fishing is discarded due to poor fishing practices and inadequate management, equivalent to 10 million tonnes of wasted fish every year.

Both types of trawling are commonly used by industrial fishing fleets, and account for 20% of fish and 25% of shellfish landed. Bottom trawling for prawn (or shrimp, as they are called in the US) is of particular concern, since it is responsible for up to half of the world's discarded catch, and up to 40% of seabed life can be removed by the pass of just one prawn trawl, taking sea life up to six years to recover. It is utterly incredible to me that anyone could have devised such a way of fishing, and that it has been used so extensively when its impacts have been so obviously devastating. Bottom trawling has been banned in an increasing number of places globally, including in European waters and in the high seas areas managed by the South Pacific Regional Fisheries Management Organisation (which accounts for 25% of the global ocean). But it still exists in the majority of international waters.

The global fishing industry is huge and growing, worth $142 billion in 2016 (nearly three times what it was worth when this book was first written). Its most significant feature is the rise in aquaculture, where fish and seafood are farmed rather than being caught wild. Aquaculture is the fastest-growing sector of all animal food production, growing from only 3.9% of fish supplies in 1970 to 48% in 2018 (84 million tonnes). On average, it has grown by 64% a year since 2009, compared with meat production, which has grown by an average of 2% per year over the past decade.

For the first time ever, over half of the fish and seafood we now buy will have been raised in fish farms, and this proportion is growing as we demand increasing amounts of fish and seafood in the face of declining wild stocks. Since salmon and prawns are two farmed species that are particularly popular in the UK and US, it is helpful to look more closely at what is involved in their production.

As we saw in 'F is for Food', salmon has moved from being a luxury to one of the cheapest of meats. In Scotland, the retail value of the salmon industry is worth £765 million a year. But this is coming at a price. One key concern is the number of chemicals that are used in salmon-rearing, including an artificial pigment to make the naturally grey flesh pink. Salmon farming is polluting because old water containing high concentrations of chemicals and fish faeces is flushed out in exchange for new. A significant problem that the salmon industry is facing (not just in Scotland but in Chile and Norway too, the other main salmon producers) is a sea lice epidemic, which is killing and damaging fish on a massive scale. The intensive conditions in which the salmon are kept are creating 'toxic toilets' which encourage such parasites and other infectious diseases to spread. This then results in huge amounts of chemicals, such as hydrogen peroxide, being used to try to fight the lice. Hydrogen peroxide is now being used in Scottish salmon farms, despite the fact that it is harmful to fish, and its use has increased from zero in 2009 to 19.6 million litres in 2015. Scottish fish farmers are now also using a toxic organophosphate called 'Split' to kill off the sea lice.

Salmon farming may have brought big economic benefits to Scotland, Chile and Norway, but if we ever want to eat it, we must ensure it is organic, or (in the UK) RSPCA-certified at least. Yes, this means it is more expensive, so let's go back to seeing salmon as a rare treat, rather than a regular on our plates.

So what about wild salmon? Sadly, the situation here is not much better, though from a different perspective. Salmon stocks in many parts of the North Atlantic are in serious decline. Many measures have been put in place to reverse this trend and restore the stocks, such as restrictive management measures and reductions in fisheries and exploitation rates. So far, however, the salmon has not responded. The only wild salmon, therefore, that we should be eating is either Pacific salmon that carries the MSC logo or Atlantic salmon that has been sustainably harvested. At all costs, we must avoid Atlantic salmon that is not able to offer that guarantee.

Above we saw the damaging effects of prawn trawling. Unfortunately, current fish farming practices are not much better. Some of the issues are similar to those regarding salmon: prawns are farmed intensively, using high levels of feed, pesticides, antibiotics and other chemicals in order to maximize profits and combat disease. The resultant pollution is horrendous. There have been improvements in this area, and the World Bank has been helping countries such as Thailand invest in effluent solutions for prawn ponds, which has reduced effluent levels going into coastal waters. Thailand has also adopted a Code of Conduct for sustainable shrimp farming and has slowed mangrove forest destruction and moved prawn ponds to outside these areas and started to replant.

However, prawns do have a high carbon footprint due to the loss of mangroves (which absorb carbon, so cutting them down both releases carbon and prevents subsequent absorption), and the short life of ponds, which leaves soil unusable for up to forty years. Incredibly, a 1 lb bag of prawns has a carbon footprint of 1 tonne of $CO_2$, ten times higher than beef produced on pasture formed from a tropical rainforest!

So what do we do with prawns? As with salmon, we should return to thinking of them as a very occasional, expensive treat. The only countries from which you can currently buy certified organic tiger, king or white prawns are Ecuador, Vietnam, India, Bangladesh and the UK. Waitrose claims that all its warm-water prawns are fully traceable back to their farm of production and that the farms are all environmentally and socially sustainable. In the US, Whole Foods sells responsibly sourced prawns and Costco sells Aquaculture Stewardship Council shrimp, but not organic ones. Whatever country of the world you live in, if you want to eat prawns/shrimp, then the onus is on you to find out which supermarkets offer well-farmed produce, and make sure they are the only ones you buy!

And this applies to all fish and seafood. Our supermarkets, at least in the UK, *are* aware of the issues raised in this chapter, and some of them are doing something about it. Aldi, Sainsbury's, Lidl, Waitrose and M&S are currently the best supermarkets in this regard. But there is a long way to go, and it is up to us as customers to tell our supermarkets that we want fish and seafood only from sustainable sources.

In the creation story we are told that God caused the water to 'teem with living creatures'. He blessed those creatures and commanded them to be 'fruitful and increase in number and fill the water in the seas' (Genesis 1:20–22). We can be extremely thankful that he did so, as there is no doubting the delight of eating those fruits of the sea, and their healthful benefits. Whether we enjoy them from the supermarket or at the restaurant, we must take responsibility to ensure that our pleasure is not working against that blessing and at the expense of God's world.

### Action points

- Load the MSC's *Pocket Good Fish Guide* app on your phone: only buy fish/seafood that is in its 'Fish to eat' list and never buy any that is in its 'Fish to avoid' list.
- Ask your supermarket (and restaurants) where the fish and seafood comes from. Congratulate them where they are getting it right, and ask them to change where they are not.

## L IS FOR LETTERS

'Oh, no! Not another one from that Mrs Valerio . . . !'

I sometimes wish I could be a fly on the wall in the customer services office at our local supermarket, because I can imagine that response as they go through their recent comments cards. I once read that we should become a nuisance to our supermarkets, asking questions about their policies and practices, and badgering them about the issues we feel are important. After all, I reason, they take so much of my money, it would be rude not to give something back in return!

So I try to let them know my concerns at every possible opportunity. Sometimes that is through the comments cards that are available at the customer services desk. I don't use them every week, but if I read something I would like to ask them about, or see something that worries me, I take a few minutes to fill in a form. Sometimes I do that online, and sometimes I'll send a tweet if I want to be more public about it. The nature of the reply depends on which particular super-market you use: whether it is positive or negative, open or defensive. As suggested in 'F is for Food', it can be interesting to ask the same question to different supermarkets and compare the responses. More often than not, the reply will lead to my writing my own reply, and soon a regular exchange over a particular issue emerges. This often leads to the query being passed on to someone from the relevant department at head office (rather than customer services), where it is dealt with directly.

Mostly I feel as if I'm banging my head against a brick wall – but not all the time. I have had some successes (most notably with Fairtrade bananas and coffee). It might just have been coincidence, but I like to think my letters and emails contributed to these policy changes.

It is easy to feel on my own, but actually this is far from the truth. When I was in the middle of a tennis game of emails with Tesco over Fairtrade bananas many years ago, a friend mentioned that she was also writing to them about the same thing. That was encouraging! Actually, I didn't realize it, but there were people all over the country putting pressure on Tesco.

'Letters' covers a number of different methods of com-munication: yes, letters, but also emails, online petitions, phone calls, postcards, comments left on Facebook pages and tweets (to company or government Twitter accounts). Campaign postcards and online petitions, in particular, have become increasingly popular, with all the main campaigning charities using them as their chief weapons. These organ-izations recognize that many people are too busy to write a proper letter. A postcard with the text already on it, which we can sign and send, is an ideal way to motivate people to do something, and to get the message across that people care about the issue at hand, though we should always remember that a letter packs more of a punch than a campaign card.

Another good way of applying pressure is to write into the readers' letters section of the local newspaper. I have heard from MPs that they keep an eye on their local paper, and if there is an issue or a campaign being talked about there, they will sit up and take notice.

Encouragingly, these methods are proving to be remarkably effective.

There have been a number of significant examples of success in the years that *L is for Lifestyle* has been in print, such as The Big Ask campaign which saw the world's first-ever climate change law brought into the UK in 2006, and people power getting the UK government to reverse its decision to sell state-owned forests in 2011. Public and faith group opposition in the US (led by 350.org) to the Keystone pipeline led to it being vetoed by President Obama (though that was overturned by President Trump).

The most recent example of success was the role that faith groups played in applying pressure for an ambitious Paris Agreement on climate change in 2015. Huge momentum was built through online petitions, postcards, letter writing, rallies, cycle rides and pilgrimages – not to mention a lot of prayer. A global petition signed by nearly 2 million people of faith calling for climate justice was presented to the then Secretary of the United Nations Framework Convention on Climate Change (UNFCC), Christiana Figueres, and President Hollande of France. It had a big impact on world leaders and decision makers attending the talks, resulting in the historic climate agreement signed by virtually all countries.

Signing online petitions, using social media, writing letters and sending emails and postcards really does make a difference. As CAFOD told me, 'Writing to politicians does have a big impact. It is the easiest way to gauge the level of public interest on one particular subject. The more postcards that land on the desks of MPs and senior politicians, the more seriously they are going to take that subject.' And this holds true for all the different channels of engagement. One thing worth noting is that it is good to personalize anything you send, so politicians know you are really speaking from your heart. They will listen to that more than if you just use a standard template. In addition, sending a card with a charity's logo on it helps the lobbying work done by that particular organization, as they then gain recognition and legitimacy through demonstrating public support.

Letters and emails *are* the most effective forms of communication, because they are personal and because they take time, and hence represent commitment to the issue. But they *do* take time, although online communication now does make life easier. I never have that time available, so somehow I have to make it. It is a good idea to set aside one evening every other month, or every three months, to be your 'campaigning evening'. Over those months, alongside the easier 'one-click' things you can do immediately, you can collect together campaign ideas and then, on that evening, sit down and work through them, doing everything in one hit. It is easy to let it slip, so make that evening sacred!

Getting involved in this kind of campaigning work is all part of being an advocate: speaking up on behalf of those who cannot speak for themselves (Proverbs 31:8–9). It is an integral part of 'spending ourselves on behalf of the hungry and satisfying the needs of the oppressed', and it works alongside the kind of lifestyle changes that we have been looking at so far. It is important and necessary work that is more than worth the time it takes to put our fingers to the keyboard.

**Action points**

- Get your diary and schedule four campaign/letter-writing evenings for the next year.
- Look back over the issues in this book and choose two topics of particular concern to you. Contact the relevant organizations and begin to get involved in their online campaigns. Many organizations allow you to subscribe to email newsletters, to 'like' their Facebook pages or to follow them on Twitter. These can be handy ways of keeping in touch and communicating your views.
- Tearfund is involved with countries all over the world in a global campaign called Renew Our World. Take a look at <http://renewourworld.net>.

# M IS FOR MONEY

It is a happy coincidence that the two central letters of the alphabet give us, in this book, the two topics of money and consumerism ('N is for Needs'). Truly, these two things are what make our world go round today. In 'I is for Investments' we looked at the particular issue of where we put the money we don't give away. In this chapter we want to look more broadly at a biblical understanding of money, and how we can respond.

In this book we are considering how we can be Christian activists, spending ourselves on behalf of the hungry, and the part our lifestyles play in this. So many of the issues involved will revolve around our understanding of money and possessions. This understanding can easily be moulded by the culture in which we live. But, as followers of Jesus, we want our understanding to be based on him, and on the rest of God's revelation in the Bible.

In 'C is for Creation' we saw how God created the world – and created it *good*. It is a totally positive account: no repudiation of the material world, but a thorough embracing of it. The fall, however, placed curses on the blessings and fullness that were there for people to enjoy.

Throughout the Old Testament, two strands appear regarding money and possessions. On the one hand, there is nothing intrinsically wrong with having either, and indeed some parts of the Old Testament see them as part of the promises of Yahweh for those who live according to his ways (e.g. Leviticus 26:3–5; Deuteronomy 28:1–14). God is seen as a God of tremendous blessing and generosity: a God who rescued his people *out* of poverty, rather than calling them *into* it! Wealth creation is a positive calling that God gives, and to be denied that ability can be a denial of God's purposes for our lives (e.g. the story of Joseph in Genesis 39:2–6; see also Proverbs 3:9–10). We have been placed in a world full of plenty, and our response should not be to reject that plenty, but rather to look after it effectively (which is why the earlier chapter on Investments is so important).

On the other hand, wealth is not necessarily seen as a reward for covenant faithfulness, and other voices in the Old Testament warn of its dangers (as is evident in the lives of many of the kings, who 'did evil in the eyes of the LORD'). Wealth in all its forms is something that shouldn't be held on to possessively, but used to serve Yahweh – something that King David certainly learned when he viewed all the Israelite people as his own possession (1 Chronicles 21). Note too that material blessing as a necessary reward from Yahweh is one strand of teaching that we do not see in the New Testament. In particular, the Old Testament makes it clear that a person's money or property should never be gained at the expense of another who is thereby left in a poorer state. The prophets provide us with a strong denunciation of the gross inequality that arose within Israel (e.g. Ezekiel 22:29; Amos 8:4–6).

When we turn to look at Jesus, we shall be disappointed if we hope to find him concerned only with individual piety. Right giving is as important to him as praying and fasting (Matthew 6), and he talks more about money than about anything else apart from the kingdom of God. He was very clear that we cannot serve both God and mammon/money (Matthew 6:24), and taught strongly about the dangers of money. He described riches as a strangler and as a worry (Luke 8:14; 12:22–34). Money can blind us to the eternal realities of life, and can indeed be a curse for us (Luke 6:20, 24; 16:19–31).

More positively, we should not be preoccupied with money because we should *seek first* the kingdom of God (Matthew 6:33). In a wonderful passage, Jesus challenges head-on our society's obsession with material things (our 'treasures', which moths and rust can destroy and thieves can steal), and instead puts before us the values of the kingdom (Matthew 6:19–34).

Jesus' message of radical kingdom economics is summed up in two incidents in the Gospels. First, Zacchaeus shows us a person who, before meeting Jesus, put all his trust and value in his wealth (Luke 19:1–9). Martin Luther once said, 'Every person needs two conversions: one of the heart and one of the wallet', and here we see these two conversions working together. Zacchaeus's money was earned at the expense of the poor people of Jericho, and he knew that the only appropriate response on meeting Jesus was to give back all that money – four times over! We can only guess at the financial effects of giving away half his possessions to the poor and then paying people back four times: it is unlikely that he would have been rich after that. Here was no giving away of his surplus; this was a radical outworking of the Jubilee principle – God's design for his people in Leviticus 25 that legislated for the cancelling of debts so that people caught in poverty (and those trapped in wealth) could start again.

The second incident in Jesus' life was his observation of the widow who gave her two very small copper coins (Luke 21:1–4). In contrast to all the wealthy people who were also putting their gifts into the temple treasury, Jesus recognized that 'this poor widow has put in more than all the others'. Again, we see how different the values of the kingdom are from the values of society. In our world, it is size and numbers that count; we are praised for the amount we give. In Jesus' eyes, what matters is how much we have left afterwards and the sacrifice that we have been prepared to make.

The early church continued Jesus' economic ethic, as the pictures given in the early chapters of Acts bear out. What is envisaged here is not the abolition of private property – clearly, people throughout the early years of the church owned their own houses and fields – but a community that put others' needs before their own, and where members were prepared to give of their own possessions and money in order to see others' needs met. The call was both to share God's blessings with his followers and not to neglect the poor with whom they came into contact.

Paul uses the collection for the church in Jerusalem as an opportunity to demonstrate that Christians' attitude towards money, and their use of it, is not a peripheral issue. In his letters we get a glimpse of the early church reaching more into the middle and upper classes.

In particular, the church at Corinth ran into problems when people expected to be able to use their wealth to buy power within the church. Paul again sets out the contrast between Jesus' way and the world's way. James picks this up, and his words contain a strong challenge for us today. Do we treat people differently according to their financial status? How does our faith outwork itself (James 2; 1 John 3:17)?

What does all this mean for us today? It means we may well need to make some changes in our attitude towards money and possessions. We shall look at this more broadly in our next chapter, but it needs stating that the biblical position is so far removed from what our culture tells us that we need continually to check ourselves and see in which camp we stand.

Of particular note here is how far we are willing even to talk about the subject. Discussing my finances is certainly something I can get prickly about. Nevertheless, I have two good friends who know all about my financial situation. Some years ago the three of us sat down and went through our budgets with one another: our monthly expenditures and incomes, our savings, our mortgages, our pensions – everything was laid out on the table and opened to one another for questioning, and as a family we are trying, slowly, to bring our financial practices and attitudes more into line with what we see in the Bible. We are far away from the ideal, and shall be working on this for the rest of our lives, but the best way we can do it is with friends around us who will question and/or support any decisions we make.

Former Director of the FBI, J. Edgar Hoover, said, 'A budget tells your money where to go, otherwise you wonder where it went.' On a practical level, one of the best things we can do is sort out our finances so that we know exactly how much money we have, what we spend, what we save and what we give away. When we do this, we can begin to see where there might be areas of weakness that we can work on, and where we might have money that we can use to help others.

This is exciting stuff! I know of one couple with a good income who live very simply. At the end of each financial year they look at what they have earned and what they have spent, and give the surplus away. One year they gave away £45,000. For others of us it might be a question of putting a small sum of money aside each month, and then giving it away when it has reached a certain amount. Perhaps we might impose on ourselves a 'luxury tax', whereby whenever we buy something that is a luxury (a bar of chocolate, a cinema ticket, even a car), we buy two and give one away, or give away the equivalent sum of money.

Whatever we do, our aim is to discipline our attitude towards money, and our use of it, to bring it into line with the Bible's teaching, so that we might use as much of it as possible to be a blessing to others.

**Action points**

- If you do not already do so, work out a budget so that you know exactly what your money is doing. The Money Charity, Christians Against Poverty and in the US Christian Credit Counselors are all good organizations that can help with this.
- Get together with a mature Christian friend and show him/her your budget. Ask your friend to comment and advise.
- Take one step that will help you use your money more for the benefit of others. When you have done that, take another step!

# N IS FOR NEEDS

A friend of mine came round to see me. As she walked in, I absentmindedly looked down at her shoes. 'Oh, don't look!' she exclaimed. 'I bought them over the weekend and I have so many pairs already. I knew I shouldn't, but once I'd seen them, I couldn't put them out of my mind till I'd got them.'

Finally she admitted, 'Ruth, I think I've got a problem. I can't stop buying things. Even when I know I shouldn't, I just give in. I've got no control over myself, and I need to get it sorted.'

My friend's confessions are nothing astounding, and would certainly be echoed by countless millions around the world – and probably by many of us reading this book too. Gandhi once said, 'There is enough in the world for man's needs, but not for man's greed.' This encapsulates the subject of this chapter: consumerism. For consumerism has taught us to blur the edges between what is a need and what is, if we are honest, just a greed.

Consumerism – the culture whereby our primary activity and focus is consuming things rather than producing them – has been specifically cultivated over the past several decades.[1] In the post-war years there was an era of mass consumption when a productivity boom led to a capacity to supply goods and services that outstripped demand. The only way to deal with this was to stimulate that demand: in other words, to produce a desire to consume. This led to all the marketing ploys with which we are now so familiar: advertising, built-in obsolescence, easy credit and the opening up of new markets such as the teenagers and the high-earning young professional market. It's amazing to think that the word 'teenager' wasn't a known category until the 1950s. For people of my age and younger who have known nothing else, it can be hard to appreciate just how much we are children of the consumer age: how different our culture is from what was before, and how we are formed and trained to consume at a high level, right from our earliest years.

When I speak on consumerism, I begin with an image of that word written in the letters of brands: the C of Coca-Cola, the S of Subway, the M of McDonald's, and so on, and ask people to identify all the brands. Generally it doesn't take long: the advertising industry does its job very effectively indeed!

One of the clear global trends while *L is for Lifestyle* has been in publication has been the inexorable rise of consumerism around the world. As we saw in 'G is for Globalization', the much-to-be-welcomed rise out of poverty has led to consumerism increasing in scale and pace. The vast majority of the world are now out of absolute poverty, and have money to buy things and emulate those of us who have already been enjoying the benefits of a consumer lifestyle and putting pressure on the planet's resources. Consumption levels for a wide variety of products (from coal to cars to coffee) are now at record levels. Of course, there is a huge disparity between the per capita consumption levels of someone in, for example, Bangladesh and someone from the UAE (which has the highest levels of household consumption in the world, with the US second and the UK twelfth), and this places even more responsibility on those of us living at a higher economic level to be consuming less.

Consumerism is not in and of itself a negative thing. As we have seen already throughout this book, we benefit from a wonderful freedom of consumer choice, and our consumption of goods can be a blessing that allows our needs to be met, as well as something that can build relationships – in *Just Living*, for example, I look at how I use my food shopping to nurture and build the relationships within my family. Bishop James Jones makes the point that 'Christianity is a religion of consumption. We are natural and original consumers. The Garden of Eden is planted with food for us to eat. And when the founder of Christianity departed this life he gave his followers an act of consumption by which to remember him.'[2] The danger though is that as we consume, so we ourselves are consumed by the ideology of consumerism that overtakes us. Consumerism can easily become the main focus of our lives, with our Christian faith something around the edges that we are using to enhance and augment the lives we have constructed for ourselves. When that happens, we have strayed into idolatry.

Consumerism is the dominant force in our society, and carries powerful values. Our identity and significance are defined by what we consume, whether that be our house, car, holiday, the latest smartphone, clothes or whatever. The advertisements all around us ensure we know the difference between the driver of a Volvo and a Renault Clio, or between a Guinness and an Absolut Vodka drinker. Thus, goods are valued for what they mean, as much as for their use, and supporting this is a whole celebrity culture in which brands pay big sums to famous people (so-called 'influencers') who will promote their brand, particularly on social media.

Consumer culture is deeply individualistic and self-centred, focused on the rights of individuals to have whatever they want and to be whatever they want. It hardly needs to be said that this has led to the expectation of instant gratification. As one credit card promises, 'It takes the waiting out of wanting.' We have lost the pleasure of gaining something we have worked hard and saved for; instead, we just put it on our credit card and get it straight away. This seems to have led us to value things less, and therefore dispose of them more easily, and so we have developed a shocking waste culture in which 'disposable' has become the norm. To counter this, I have a rule that if I see something I want to buy, I have to wait twenty-four hours. Chances are, by that time, the desire to buy it has gone, and so I leave it.

Holding pride of place is money. Without it one cannot consume, and so money is endlessly presented as having the ability to bring status, power, freedom and hence that elusive prize: happiness. Indeed, happiness is what it's all about. Consumerism is, at its heart, the ultimate pursuit of happiness and fulfilment. It offers us a life in which nothing goes wrong. The road is always empty, the dish is always full, the colours are always bright, the clothes are always white, the hair is always perfect and the man nearly so . . .

We may laugh at this, but the reality is that consumerism has come at a price, and has affected the most important areas of our lives. This includes religion. People shop around to find the religion, or church, that fits them best. Commitment is at an all-time low: if it doesn't suit our needs, we move on somewhere else. Consumerism affects our faith, and the danger for us is that we develop a compartmentalized Christianity that makes no connection between our faith on a Sunday morning and how we spend our money the rest of the week. Tom Wright warns of a Christianity that becomes 'focused on me and my survival, my sense of God, my spirituality, rather than outwards on God, and on God's world that still needs the kingdom-message so badly'.[3]

The global picture of consumerism – as we have seen already throughout this book – is of a world of finite resources struggling to meet the demand for more, more, more. There are many causes of poverty: personal choices, disasters, lack of technology, Western colonialism, corruption and so on, but we have to recognize that our high levels of consumerism are a key part of our world's unjust structures.

However, we must always remember that we have a choice! We *can* choose how we live our lives and how we spend our money. And, alongside cutting down our consumption, we have already seen that when we do consume, we have the power to do so in a way that actually helps alleviate poverty and reduce environmental destruction.

In 'M is for Money' we looked in depth at what the Bible teaches about money and possessions, all of which is of course relevant here too. What else does the Bible say that speaks into our culture? A key Old Testament law is the Sabbath. This laid down important principles regarding rest and trusting God. It speaks to our culture of incessant work, reminding us that our work is not the be-all and end-all, and that *we* are not the be-all and end-all. It confirms that rather than economic achievement, our relationship with God, with one another and with our world is at the heart of what it means to be human, and hence is our ultimate destiny.

Matthew 6 is a passage that speaks directly to our situation. What do we put our security in? Is it in God's provision or our material possessions? Which is more important to us? What are we investing in for the long term? Do we have an eternal perspective when we consider these things? How important are clothes and food to us? Do we 'run after these things' rather than the kingdom of God?

An overriding biblical theme that is so important for us to recover today is that of contentment. Consumerism makes us think we need more and more, creating a continual dissatisfaction that is temporarily expunged by an online order. Its message is that we are not rich enough, beautiful enough or smart enough. In direct opposition, the voices of the Bible tell us to be content: 'Keep your lives free from the love of money and be content with what you have' (Hebrews 13:5; see also Philippians 4:11–12 and 1 Timothy 6:6–10). Contentment comes from being secure in the knowledge that money and possessions are not the focus of our lives: that honour belongs to Jesus alone.

In Philippians 4:11–12, Paul talks of being content whatever the circumstances: not just knowing when to say that we have enough, but being content even when things are hard. A positive understanding of suffering is needed, since we are bombarded with messages that tell us that it is our right to be healthy and wealthy and beautiful, and that personal fulfilment is based on these things. The reality of the Christian life is that Jesus promises no such thing. The Bible often represents the life of faith as a hard, an unrewarding and even a painful experience, and Jesus speaks of it as a cross. Rather than expecting to experience a carefree life with no suffering, Christians can expect instead to find the grace and strength to go through these difficulties, knowing that ultimately they are victorious in Christ.

Romans 12:1–2 urges, 'Do not conform to the pattern of this world, but be transformed by the renewing of your mind.' Nowhere is this more germane than in this chapter.

As followers of Jesus, we live by a story different from that told by our culture. We know we do not need to be surrounded by 'stuff' in order to find fulfilment. As we simplify our lives and refuse to be shackled by the chains of consumerism, we shall discover a new sense of joy and liberation.

**Action points**

- Sort through your clothing, kitchen cupboards or even your whole house (!) and box up anything that you don't need or use. If after three months you have not opened the box at all, give its contents away. For example, you could donate them to a charity shop, hold a swishing party (where you swap clothes), offer them free online or sell them at a car boot sale and give away the money.
- Watch *The Story of Stuff*, <https://storyofstuff.org>, and support the movement to buy less.
- Join local green groups and networks that encourage produce sharing or freecycling rather than buying new.
- When you go shopping, take this list of questions with you:
  1. Do I really need this product? Why?
  2. Is this an impulsive purchase or have I planned it?
  3. Have I done research to find the best product to meet my needs?
  4. Do I know the environmental consequences of this purchase?
  5. Does this product meet Fairtrade standards?
  6. Can I borrow the equivalent? Buy it and share it with someone? Buy it second hand?

7. Was it made or grown locally, thereby saving energy and packing?

## Notes

1. This is putting consumerism at its simplest. For a much more detailed look at consumerism (including its positive sides) and how it functions in our society, see Ruth Valerio, *Just Living: Faith and Community in an Age of Consumerism* (Hodder & Stoughton, 2016).
2. James Jones, *Jesus and the Earth* (SPCK, 2003), p. 25.
3. N. T. Wright, *For All God's Worth: True Worship and the Calling of the Church* (Eerdmans, 2014), pp. 63–64.

# O IS FOR ORGANIC

'Didn't we do this already in "F is for Food"?' In our chapter on food we did indeed begin to look at the reasons for buying and eating more organic produce, but there is more to consider. I want to look further at organic food in this chapter, as well as move it beyond this issue alone.

The one factor, in the UK at least, that always comes up alongside this subject is price, as organic produce is often more expensive than non-organic. Why is this the case? We need to ask ourselves first: why is non-organic food so cheap? One reason is farming subsidies. Currently (though this may well change in a post-Brexit world), EU CAP subsidies are primarily based on the number of hectares farmed, plus additional direct payments given for implementing green measures. Big non-organic farms therefore receive far greater subsidies than organic farms, which tend to be smaller (eighty-three hectares smaller on average).

The second reason is that the external costs created by intensive farming are paid for by the consumer. These costs include those of cleaning up rivers contaminated by chemicals (which is then reflected in our water bills), repairing wildlife habitats, and coping with sickness and disasters caused by farming, such as the bovine TB epidemic which was primarily caused by cattle-to-cattle transmission and exacerbated by intensive farming and transportation. (This has so far cost the UK taxpayer £500 million, according to TB Free England, excluding culling, which has cost another £50 million.) Although prosecution for environmental damage has become more likely since the first edition of this book was launched, serious breaches of pollution legislation are on the rise, especially from large, intensive farms.

A 2017 report, 'True Cost Accounting in Farming and Finance', co-sponsored by Triodos Bank, showed cheap, non-organic food to contain substantial 'hidden costs' to our health and society, including negative impacts on climate, biodiversity, water use and soils. The conclusion they reached was that costs outweigh the benefits of cheap food by $4.8 trillion every year! It is often said that the consumer pays for their food twice: once at the till and twice through their taxes with the clean-up costs (and we could add a third time, when we pay for it with our health). When you factor in these external costs, organic food saves not only money but also carbon emissions, soil fertility and water.

The third reason why non-organic food is so cheap is that cheapness is what we expect and demand. In the first edition of this book I stated how, over the past thirty years, the percentage of our household budget spent on food had dropped, on average, from 24% to 16%. Now this percentage has dropped to just around 10%. We then choose to spend that money on other items, and the average household now spends more money on leisure goods and services than on food and non-alcoholic drinks. Quantity rather than quality is thus what we have been given, and our supermarkets are in a constant battle with their rivals to give us the food we want, as cheaply as they can.

Having considered the cost of cheap food, we then need to look at what goes into organic farming. To put it at its simplest, organic food is more expensive because it is more labour-intensive to farm without chemicals; the yields are often lower, and parts of the farm lie fallow each year to increase fertility, and so cannot generate an income. The conversion process can be an expensive time; the farmer cannot charge the premium price for organic produce, yet the yields will be lower and the initial expenses higher. What results from this process, however, is farms that observe a high standard of animal welfare, with crop rotation, strong environmental practices and the use of skilled techniques rather than a dependence on chemicals.

The cost of buying organic – which can be as much as 50% more expensive – can be hard to swallow for those of us wanting to support its development. When you consider the illusion involved in our so-called cheap food, and then look at what goes into organic farming, however, there can be no doubt that organic food is worth the extra.

Many people now realize that being organic reaches beyond food alone. In the EU, around 320 million tonnes of chemicals are produced each year, with potentially as many as 20,000 different ones being used, though that figure is unclear. There is much disagreement too over how many chemicals are in use today in the US, with the chemical industry saying 7,700 different chemicals are in use, whereas the NRDC (National Resources Defense Council) puts the figure at over 80,000.

What we know is that chemicals are in everything we buy: sofas, computers, TVs, detergents, paints, mattresses, toys, windows, tins and so on. There is no doubt that the chemical industry contributes to our quality of life, and we could not live the life we do without the use of many of these chemicals. Under the EU's Regulation on Registration, Evaluation, Authorisation and Restriction of Chemicals (REACH), the testing of chemicals for their impact on health and the environment has now got much stricter, and no chemical can now go on to the market unless it has been tested. However, even the EU admits that some chemicals do harm health, and there has been a rise in health problems related to chemicals, most obviously asthma and skin irritations, but also potential long-term damage such as cancer and hormone disruption, the links with which are still being explored.

The drive towards organic is about reducing our exposure to these chemicals, and this reaches into every area of our lives. Here are three of the most important.

If organic food is a concern, the next logical step is to extend that into our *gardening* practices: there is little point in supporting organic developments if you scatter slug pellets over your flowerbeds and douse your plants in insecticide! Gardening brings some of the most satisfying pleasures of life. What better way to garden than in a way that enhances the small ecosystem you have charge over, encouraging birds, bees and butterflies, and providing space for local wildlife?

Another area is *cleaning products*. These are full of chemicals, some very harmful both to the environment and to our health. Thankfully, there are now very good environmentally friendly products readily available in supermarkets and health food shops. When we know about the damaging effects of regular cleaners, how can we not use these products instead?

As always, they can be slightly more expensive. If this is a particular concern, go back to basics and make your own cleaning solutions: bicarbonate of soda and lemon juice, for example, do a great job.

A third area is *beauty products*. According to the Women's Environmental Network, the average UK woman uses twenty different skin products every day, many of which are simply a mix of lots of chemicals (take a look at the ingredients and see for yourself!). Perfume also can contain up to 30% of substances that are toxic and not regulated. The 'cocktail effect' of all these chemicals in combination is not fully understood, and many products contain ingredients that are harmful to human health, such as parabens (a preservative) and phthalates (a solvent). I decided some while ago that if I didn't want to eat chemicals, then I didn't want to put them on my skin or use them on my hair and teeth either. As with cleaning, so also with beauty products: there are alternatives to buy and recipes to make, and I have had great fun finding out about them and experimenting.

Becoming more organic is part of developing a lifestyle that takes more care of ourselves and of the world that God has made. The Old Testament makes it clear that respect for the land that God has given us is an integral part of our relationship with him and with one another. The encouraging news is that, as Michael van Straten says, every step does make a difference:

> Every family that encourages a household culture of organic living makes an even greater difference, by educating their children to live organically in the future. Every tiny saving of fuel and every purchase of organic food will help. Each of these small steps contributes to a reduction of toxic material in our environment and a lower rate of global warming.[1]

**Action points**

- Find out more about the issues around organics by contacting the organizations involved in its promotion, such as the Soil Association and Garden Organic.
- Get online help on the best cleaning and beauty products to buy, from organizations such as the Organic Consumer Association and Environmental Working Group (EWG) in the US and the Women's Environmental Network in the UK. And check out the Green Living posts on ethical beauty and cleaning on my website.
- Read books such as *Skin Deep* to learn more about what's in your cosmetics.[2]
- Choose one food product, one cleaning product and one beauty product, and change them to organic and/or home-made.

**Notes**

1. Michael van Straten, *Organic Living* (Rodale Books, 2001), p. 15.
2. Pat Thomas, *Skin Deep: The Essential Guide to What's in the Toiletries and Cosmetics You Use* (Rodale, 2008).

# P IS FOR PLASTIC[1]

This week I met with an MP who decided to do a plastic-free Lent. She got forty-one other MPs in her party involved, and it made a good, positive media story. Unknown to her, the Church of England decided to do something similar, spearheaded by the Bishop of Dudley, and totally unaware this was being planned, I also took Lent to focus on breaking my plastic habits.

I decided to do plastic-*less* Lent rather than plastic-free, as trying to go plastic-free feels an impossible, daunting task, and I wanted to do something that was encouraging and motivating and didn't make me (or anyone else) feel as if I'd failed at the first hurdle (plus, who doesn't like a bit of alliteration?). We thought we'd do it mostly as a family, but I put up a page on Facebook for anyone else who wanted to join me . . . and before I knew it, there were 3,000 of us, from fifty-five countries, all wanting to take steps forward together to reduce our plastic usage. Amazing![2]

Of course, we mustn't forget that plastic serves many positive functions. It is needed in medicine, it helps food last longer and so reduces food waste, and its use in our domestic appliances makes them lighter and so both reduces transportation emissions and makes them more suitable to use at home. Plastic is in virtually every aspect of our modern living (even chewing gum contains plastic – and tea bags and make-up!), and I don't think any of us would really want to go back to the time when plastic didn't exist.

But we are using way too much of it and it is petroleum-based, which is what we need to be moving away from. Too much of what we do employ is used only once and then thrown away, and we don't have the infrastructure to dispose of it properly once we have stopped using it. In fact, this is the biggest problem with plastic: it is actually impossible to dispose of. Once it exists, it is around for hundreds and sometimes thousands of years, and even then it simply breaks down into smaller and smaller particles (microplastics), which are now causing even more problems further down the line, particularly in our seas.

Once we begin to look at the reality of the situation, it is quite overwhelming. One of the symptoms of globalization is a supply chain that needs plastic to make it work (to protect and extend the life of goods), and so every year an estimated 335 million metric tonnes of plastic are produced, and this is set to double by 2035. Estimates suggest that by 2025, lower-middle income countries' plastic waste will triple, and upper-middle income countries' plastic waste will double, as their economies and populations grow. We are all well aware of the problem of plastic bags (called 'the national flower' in India because of the way they adorn trees and bushes), but one recently emerged variation is plastic sachets, particularly in Asia and Africa, that cater for families who can't afford standard sizes of products (e.g. shampoo and toothpaste). Smaller and therefore cheaper sachets allow them to access such products. But they are a waste nightmare, and have become a massive problem.

The problems caused by such a huge volume of plastic in our world are, of course, immense. Marine plastic pollution is now well documented, with shocking images of vast floating islands of plastic, turtles trapped in plastic fishing nets, and other marine life found dead with plastic bags and other bits inside them. The majority of marine plastic pollution comes from the land: from blow-off from coastal communities and industry, and also from rivers carrying inland waste down to the sea. Where there aren't proper waste management systems, plastic waste builds up in streets and gets washed or blown into waterways, and is eventually carried down to the seas. Our marine ecosystems are being devastated by plastic, and we urgently need to tackle it.

Plastic pollution is also hugely problematic for the people who live with it – and, as always, that is people in poverty. Some years ago I spent time in the slums in Chennai, India, and visited homes next to a river. The river was filthy: full of waste, both plastic and human, and big rats ran around us. When it rained, the waste built up and clogged the river, which would flood and seep into the dwellings. Such conditions are a breeding ground for water-borne diseases such as cholera, and rat-related diseases such as the plague and typhus. Waste plastic items can collect pools of water, thus making them breeding grounds for malaria and dengue-carrying mosquitoes.

Where there is no effective waste management system, people often resort to burning waste to get rid of it (and sometimes even use it as a cooking fuel). We will look at large-scale incineration more in 'R is for Recycling', but this localized plastic burning is extremely damaging to health, leading to respiratory problems and cardiovascular disease. A study in Ethiopia found that children living in slums with uncollected waste were six times more likely to suffer from acute respiratory infections than those living in households receiving regular collections.

It is shocking to think that around 3 billion people have no proper waste management! This is one of the clearest examples of the need to tackle poverty and planet together. If we could both reduce the amount of plastic produced and help people benefit from effective waste management, we would improve lives *and* help stop plastic entering into the marine system.

So what needs to happen? We need governments and global institutions, businesses and individuals all to act together.

Governments must put into place those policies that encourage good practice for businesses and individuals, such as bans on plastic bags and disposable coffee cups and increased penalties for using non-recyclable packaging. We could call on our governments to follow the example of Costa Rica, which is aiming to be single-use plastic-free by 2021, to provide better recycling facilities (as we will see in 'R is for Recycling'), to put in place robust Marine Litter Action Plans and to ensure that plastic remains firmly on the international political agenda. And we can encourage our governments to help poorer countries, both financially and technically, to develop good waste management systems.

Businesses must take responsibility for their plastic use and the whole lifecycle of their products, moving away from a linear model of extract, use, dispose, to a circular one that has recyclability built into the product. Innovative design is key to this, as is the potential to move away from plastic to alternative materials (e.g. for packaging and clothing – though also being careful about what is switched to). Moving away from disposable or even recyclable packaging to what can be refilled and reused is also important, and tackling the 'sachet economy' is going to be crucial. As one of the big culprits in this area, Unilever is encouragingly taking steps to do this.

And, as individuals, alongside getting involved in campaigns to push our governments and corporations to change, we can take our own steps to reduce the amount of plastic in our lives. From food to beauty products, to clothes to cleaning products . . . there is so much we can do.

Let me finish this chapter with two examples that show how ordinary people can make a big difference in their local communities.

Rosemary had never protested publicly until plans to build a massive incinerator near her home were announced. Believing that burning waste is to be prevented at all costs, and that much more can be done to reduce, reuse and recycle (and having read *L is for Lifestyle* when it first came out!), Rosemary joined a small local protest near the proposed incinerator site with a few others. Before long she and her family were handing out Stop the Incinerator flyers and asking residents to sign a petition which she helped deliver to the county council. Facts about similar developments being fought elsewhere were added to the anti-incinerator Facebook page. After an intense campaign period, Rosemary was present at the committee meeting at which all the hard work was vindicated: the incinerator application was refused. Now she is involved with a host of things locally, aimed at improving recycling rates and reducing food waste.

Maria lives in a poor neighbourhood in the city of Recife, Brazil. Her home is by a river which can flood up to nine times a year, coming into her home because of the vast amounts of plastic clogging it up. She even saw the dead body of her neighbour float by her home, and that was when she knew she needed to do something. So she started collecting plastic bottles. These she sells to a litter collector, and she has joined the work of Instituto Solidare, set up by the local Baptist church with support from Tearfund. Together they work to clear up the river, and have set up an artisan cooperative helping women turn the plastic waste into products. And they also petitioned the state government, which has led to some clearance being done. There is so much more to be done, but real progress is being made.

Two women. Two stories. But the impact goes far beyond them.

**Action points**

- Buy a reusable water bottle and coffee cup, and get into the habit of taking them with you so that you never need to use disposable ones again.
- Tearfund has done excellent work in the area of plastics and poverty, and around the idea of the circular economy (which comes into Tearfund's bigger vision of a fully *restorative* economy). It is currently running a plastic campaign, so take a look and get involved.
- The next time you buy a product with unnecessary packaging, contact the company and ask them to stop. Get into the habit of doing this regularly, demonstrating that there is real consumer desire for change.

## Notes

1. I owe a huge debt to the amazing Tearfund Advocacy Team for the content of this chapter, and particularly to Joanne Green, Senior Policy Advisor, who has spearheaded Tearfund's pioneering work on plastic and the link between plastic and poverty. The source material for this chapter comes from internal briefings and articles at <https://learn.tearfund.org>.

2. The plastic-less Lent group was so successful that people asked for it to continue beyond Lent, so it is now called Plastic-Less Living and you can find it easily on Facebook, with lots of great ideas and conversations being generated.

# Q IS FOR QUESTIONS

The Girl Guides have brought out a Media Critic badge, to encourage girls to learn about the media and ask questions about what they see and hear. Maybe we should all work towards earning it! I hope this book will encourage all of us to keep asking questions, because questions are what keep us moving forward; they keep changing us; they push boundaries and revolutionize situations. To be someone who asks questions is to be someone who is not content with the status quo. Asking questions changes businesses, governments and the law, as well as ourselves. The US economist Paul Samuelson said that 'good questions outrank easy answers', and we must be prepared to fight against those who will try to satisfy us with easy answers. We live in a world of confusion, with soundbites, populist rhetoric and hyperbole, 'fake news' and polarized debates, exacerbated by the way we engage with social media, surrounding ourselves with friends and followers who think like us, and shouting angrily at anyone coming from a different perspective. It is so important that we don't just accept what we are told (yes, even in this book), that we find ways to do our own research and thinking, and that we listen and ask questions, both of those we agree with and those we disagree with, in order to keep learning.

In this chapter I want to look at a question that I am *always* asked when I am speaking on the sorts of issues in this book, one that has been hinted at elsewhere, but would benefit from being considered further. And, as we will see, this good question has indeed no easy answers.

It is what I call the 'green-beans-from-Kenya' question: that is, should we buy green beans from Kenya (for example) in order to help poor farmers, or should we *not* buy them, in order to reduce the environmental impacts of the food chain and help the environment?[1]

Let us look at the different sides of the debate.

On the one side are those who say that we should always shop as locally as possible, encouraging trade to operate primarily on a localized basis rather than internationally. This is not to say that we should never buy from overseas, as clearly there are some goods that we simply can't grow in the countries that many of us come from (coffee, bananas, cocoa, etc.), but is more a case of when local is available and in season, that is what we should go for. This has a number of advantages. First, of course, is the benefit environmentally, as food does not have to travel huge distances to reach our plates, hence reducing the impact of long-distance food transportation with its heavy use of fuel, and subsequently our contribution to climate change. On a more subtle level, I found that when I started buying some of my food more locally, it strengthened my understanding of food, and was a big contributor in getting me more engaged in ecological issues.

Local food will often be fresher, and therefore tastier and more nutritious, and it encourages food diversity and smaller, less intensive farms, as well as requiring less plastic packaging. Concentrating on local also helps with issues of food security and our long-term ability to feed ourselves, whatever country we are reading this in, particularly as we know we are eventually going to face disruptions to global food production due to our warming world.

From the perspective of the 'poor farmers in Kenya', food security applies here too, as it is argued that they are better off growing their own food for their own people, and not relying on the vagaries of the global market and the vulnerability that comes from dependence on a few export crops. Such crops are generally intensively grown and contribute to water scarcity, and can cause big problems when a local product suddenly becomes a popular 'superfood' in economically developed countries, becoming too expensive for the local people (as has happened with quinoa and asparagus in South America). As with local communities in the economically developed countries, so too a greater emphasis on local food production would encourage people in Kenya to have more responsibility for their communities, rather than being at the mercy of global fiscal policies. People everywhere, including those from poorer countries, should be encouraged to engage in making a living from things that they, or people in their geographical area, *need*, not what people in the rich world *want*. There is a recognition here that we have made communities in poorer countries dependent on us, and therefore we have to take most of the responsibility for working to help such countries implement transition schemes so that they can change to working to fulfil their own basic needs.

However, on the other side are those who say that stopping buying beans from Kenya would deprive the Kenyan farmers of a livelihood that they desperately need. According to the UN's International Civil Aviation Organization and the African Airlines Association (AFRAA), the export of fresh fruit and vegetables to the UK provides £35 million to the Kenyan economy, and over 1 million rural African livelihoods are supported by the UK consumption of air-freighted fruit and vegetables. The UK is the single biggest export market for Kenyan fruit and vegetables, and the market for exported Kenyan horticultural products (fruit, vegetables and flowers), which is largely air-freighted, is currently growing at 10% per year. To put it bluntly, while we may dream of localized economies, the consequences of our unequal world mean that less developed countries simply *have* to export to the richer countries in order to make money to survive and develop.

What's more, the statistics on food miles are not always as straightforward as they may seem, and it is generally the case that a food product grown in a low-income country will use less energy than that same one grown *out of season* in a high-income country. For example, roses grown in Kenya *and flown to the UK* use almost six times less $CO_2$ than roses grown in greenhouses in Holland, demonstrating that food miles are as concerned with the methods of production as with the mode and distance of transportation.

People on this side of the debate also point out that food miles associated with the export of fresh fruit and vegetables from sub-Saharan Africa equate to only 0.1% of the UK's entire carbon emissions, and that if we are concerned with reducing our emissions, there are other more significant steps we could take instead, such as reducing our meat consumption.

It is obvious, therefore, that this issue is far from clear, and the debates around it will continue for a long while yet. What makes it harder still is that statistics on methods of production, mode of transportation and overall $CO_2$ emissions from any given product are not easy to come by, nor are the facts as to how many pence per product the producer receives. These details are certainly not printed on the product in the supermarket when you are holding it in your hand and trying to decide whether or not to buy it!

For me, this is part of the reality of living in a fallen world: a 'world of wounds',[2] in which often the choices we have to make are not perfect. This whole area is extremely complex, and also one in which our choices will be determined by our own individual priorities. We each need to determine what our priorities are, and then, to the best of our knowledge, decide when local or air-freighted food supports those. It is worth noting here that shipped products have a lower carbon footprint than those that have been flown, though still a higher footprint than our local produce.

Questions, questions, questions. So often there are no easy answers, but we must keep asking them nonetheless, and often, simply in that act of asking, we find a way to take another step forward.

**Action points**

- Don't stop asking questions, especially ones such as 'Do I really need this?' and 'Is that really the case?'
- Support organizations such as Factcheck.org and Snopes.com that help uncover media and political falsehoods.
- Take a look at the Gapminder website.

**Notes**

1. Another example I could have used for this question would have been pots of chopped tropical fruit in the fresh fruit aisle of our supermarkets.

2. Aldo Leopold, *A Sand County Almanac* (OUP USA, 1968), p. 197, cited in Steven C. Bouma-Prediger, *For the Beauty of the Earth: A Christian Vision for Creation Care* (Baker Academic, 2010), p. 16. The full quote is: 'One of the penalties of an ecological education is that one lives alone in a world of wounds.'

# R IS FOR RECYCLING

I went on holiday many years ago to Indonesia to see my brother who was living there. We had a wonderful time travelling across the Indonesian islands. One of my most vivid memories was crossing from one island to another on a large local boat. There were quite a few bins on board, which people diligently used. As we drew near to the shore, I leaned over the side of the boat to take in the view ahead: stunning white beach, clear blue coralled sea, coconut palms lining the beach – and watched as, to my horror, the crew took all the bins and, one by one, tipped their contents into the sea!

In 'P is for Plastic' we looked at the issues around plastic waste, all of which are relevant here too, but waste in general is a problem facing all of us, wherever we live in the world. Globally, we produce somewhere between 7 billion and 10 billion tonnes of waste each year, and this is growing as both population and economies grow. Many of us might like to think we are too sophisticated to tip our rubbish into the sea so blatantly, but before we criticize those Indonesian boatmen, let's turn our focus on to our own waste habits.

In the UK, about 195 million tonnes of waste is produced every year – 27.3 million tonnes, or 14% of total UK waste, comes from households, and the average person currently throws away their body weight in municipal waste (i.e. waste that is collected by local authorities) every two months! The good news is that waste figures in the UK have fallen dramatically over the past couple of decades, with the government bringing in increasingly stricter policies that have made the biggest waste-producing industries reduce the amount they generate. In the US the figures aren't so encouraging, with consumers throwing away more than 262 million tonnes of waste every year (an increase of 26% between 1960 and 2015). According to the EPA, this is equivalent to nearly 4.5 lb of rubbish being thrown away per person, per day in the US!

Like the Indonesian boatmen, we can easily feel this rubbish has disappeared and we need no longer think about it. But this couldn't be further from the truth: there is no such thing as throwing our rubbish *away*.

Just under half (48%) of UK rubbish is buried in landfill tips (compared to 53% of US rubbish). This is a massive drop from when the first edition of this book was launched fifteen years ago when just under 90% of waste went to landfill! In the UK, huge and very welcome progress has also been made in managing landfill sites, with strict controls to ensure there is no significant risk to health or the local environment, though that doesn't stop them producing $CO_2$ and methane as the rubbish biodegrades, which of course contribute to climate change. A key change over recent decades though is that more than two times more waste is now being incinerated in the UK rather than landfilled. This is because the UK is literally running out of landfill space.

Incineration is a hotly debated topic. Done badly, at low cost with little control, it is harmful both to the environment and to health, releasing dangerous pollutants and toxins into the air. It can also undermine councils' recycling schemes because it demands a constant supply of waste in order to be economic. Some councils have even had to bring in waste from other areas and abandon their plans for waste reduction and recycling. Done well, though, it can be a good alternative to landfill (but never an alternative to recycling), especially when used to turn waste into energy. The best types, which have strict pollution controls, are very expensive – they can cost $500 million – but they can have their place in a sustainable waste management system.

*Alternative Energy News* places incineration fourth in the hierarchy of how to deal with waste, alongside other energy-recovering solutions such as composting and anaerobic digestion. Fifth, and bottom, is landfill. And the first three? It won't surprise you to hear it's the old-fashioned mantra: Reduce, Reuse, Recycle.

**Reduce**

The economist E. F. Schumacher said, 'We tolerate a high rate of waste and then try to cope with the problem of recycling. Would it not be more intelligent first of all to try and reduce the rate of waste? The recycling problem may then itself become much more manageable.'[1] We should try at every possible opportunity to reduce the amount we use, and hence the amount we throw away. As a general rule, anything with the label 'disposable' should be avoided, and we should always try to buy things to last.

A lot of our rubbish comes in the form of packaging. Despite initially being a leader in this area, Germany is now the top trash producer, per capita, in Europe. It is introducing new packaging legislation at the time of writing, with far higher packaging recycling targets for different materials by 2022, including a 70% target for reusable beverage packaging. Buying locally produced food from local outlets is often the best way of reducing the packaging we buy, as supermarkets so often go overboard in this area, particularly with processed food. If you have the nerve, take off all the unnecessary packaging on products you buy and leave it at the checkout, or preferably with the shop manager. And then ask the manager to introduce plastic- and packaging-free aisles. Of course, following 'N is for Needs', the fewer things we buy, the less packaging we will use.

One little-discussed aspect is sanitary protection: the plastic and cardboard packaging and the non-organic cotton and plastic used for its production. According to Natracare, most sanitary pads are 90% plastic and one pack is equivalent to four plastic bags. In the UK over 3 billion sanitary towels, tampons and panty liners are bought every year, and approximately 700,000 panty liners, 2.5 million tampons and 1.4 million sanitary towels are flushed down the toilet in the UK every single day. An estimated 2 million of these items wind up on the UK shoreline. Speaking to the women here, if you want to use disposable products, at least make sure they are from organic cotton and you put them in the bin. Much better still though is to use a menstrual cup and/or washable knickers and pads. Go on . . . you can do it!

As you open your eyes to the issue of packaging, you may begin to notice practices of governments, councils and businesses – both locally and nationally – that go against the principle of reducing waste. Your local council recycling officer, your MP or government minister, and shop managers are good people to whom to voice your concerns.

**Reuse**

In our disposable culture it seems so much more natural to throw something away rather than consider how we might reuse it and thereby prevent wasting resources and energy on a new product. Plastic bags have been the classic example, but the charges on carrier bags across the UK, introduced from 2011 in Wales to 2015 in England, have had a big impact, reducing usage by around 80%. Following on from the Action point in 'P is for Plastic', the big culprits now are single-use water bottles and disposable coffee cups. In the UK we use 2.5 billion cups, and the US uses more than 16 billion disposable coffee cups with 25 billion Styrofoam cups being thrown away every year! At the Tearfund office in England we were shocked to discover that we got through 13,000 cups in six months (yes, really!), and that was enough for us to take the decision to stop using them and invest in washable mugs.

If you have young children, an area where you can make a vast difference is by choosing reusable nappies. Currently, disposable nappies account for 3% of household waste, and this has become one of the major waste issues, with 8 million disposable nappies thrown away every day in the UK. Each nappy uses a lot of energy and resources in production, and can take up to 500 years to decompose. Washing nappies is not the hassle that parents using 'disposables' tend to think it is. I used washables for both my children, and then passed the set on to a friend who used them for her three. What a huge saving of money and resources!

**Recycle**

Finally, when we have reduced and reused as much as possible, we can recycle (and remember too to buy recycled – that helps stimulate the demand). Recycling is far more efficient in terms of energy and resources than landfilling or incinerating, and reduces the habitat damage caused by the extraction of raw materials. It also helps us take more responsibility for the waste that we produce, and is good at job creation: the Environmental Services Association and WRAP estimate that 10,000 new jobs could be created in the UK if the government went for more recycling and efficient resource use.

Almost everything we use can be recycled: our kitchen and garden waste, paper, glass, plastic, cans, foil, textiles, furniture, other household goods, batteries, wood, oil and tyres. Many of these we can dispose of easily through composting, recycling bins and kerb-side collection schemes. Other items may take more time and investigation (<www.wastepoint. co.uk> or <www.recycle-more.com> are good sites to visit). There may yet be some recyclable waste for which there are no local facilities. If this is the case, then ask your council to provide them.

The UK recycling record has been steadily improving, and we now recycle around 45% of household waste, overtaking the US where 34% of waste is recycled. However, household recycling rates have remained fairly static since 2010, and the UK is unlikely to hit its 50% recycling target by 2020. At the time of writing, the UK recycling system is in crisis because China has now closed its doors to taking many forms of waste for recycling (historically the UK sent a lot of its recycling to China), and there are not the checks in place to ensure proper recycling in the countries to which it is now being sent. There is a need for the UK government both to put in place stringent controls when it sends its recycling overseas, and also to develop its own coherent recycling infrastructure. The current system is hugely complicated, with each council doing things differently and causing confusion for residents. The government is working on a resource and waste strategy, and we wait to see what it says. In the meantime, it reinforces the need for us to reduce and reuse, and to call on the UK government to sort out this mess.

All of this is our responsibility and part of how we take care of God's creation. After all, there is no such thing as waste in nature – the output from one organism is the input for another. As part of nature, we too can take steps to make waste an irrelevant concept.

**Action points**

- Look at what goes into your bin. What is its highest content? Take steps to reduce that.
- Next time you go round the supermarket, make a note of all the excess packaging and unnecessary plastic and cans you see. Contact your supermarket online or in person, listing it all and asking them to reduce it and change their usage.
- Find out about the recycling facilities in your area. Are there gaps? If so, ask your council to fill them.
- Support WasteAid, WRAP and other anti-waste organizations and zero-waste campaigns.

**Note**

1. Quoted in James Odgers and Ruth Valerio, *Simplicity, Love and Justice* (Alpha International, 2004), p. 52.

# S IS FOR SIMPLICITY

It feels very apt that I am working on this chapter while away at the Taizé community in France. An ecumenical monastic community, it has become known for its particular style of musical chants and its focus on peace and justice, prayer and meditation. Set in the stunning countryside of south Burgundy, it attracts around 75,000 visitors a year. I am sitting at a little table in a basic room, with no decorations and just a bed and some clothes hanging space (yes, I know even that is luxury for Taizé!), lit up by the open window. I am speaking at a week for eighteen- to thirty-five-year-olds and taking space to write while I am here. The brothers own nothing themselves, and accept no donations or inheritances.

For many of us, that might be what we think of when we hear the word 'simplicity'. Or maybe we think of decluttering and minimalism, of modern living in a white space with everything tidied away out of sight. Whatever comes to mind, I believe simplicity is an idea that has much to teach us as we think about how to live in ways that respect and take care of this world and its inhabitants.

Henry Thoreau, one of the great writers on this issue, said, 'A person is rich in proportion to the things he can leave alone.' Simplicity is about discovering what it really means to be rich, rather than seeing wealth as being all about money, and it's about an internal attitude (the things we *can* leave alone), as much as it is about the external things that we do.

Simplicity is about our choices. As we look at our lives, do we know how we've ended up living how we're living, and why? What choices have we made that control our present lifestyle? When we wanted that new house or car, were we aware that the trade-off would mean working longer hours to pay for them, and seeing less of the people we love? Too often we find ourselves on the treadmill of life, paying the consequences for choices we hardly knew we were making at the time. What stage of life are you at, and what choices could you make now that might open up new pathways of possibility?

Simple living is about stopping that treadmill and giving us the space to choose how we want to live our lives. There are many voices around us that tell us happiness is to be found in good clothes and nice jewellery; in a job that commands respect; in crashing out in front of the TV in order to recover, with your phone in one hand; in having a busy diary. Simplicity asks us to sit and listen to those other whispers inside us that we seldom have the time to hear. It helps us discover the happiness that comes not from having an abundance of money and things, but from having space for intimacy in our friendships, space for ourselves, space to live in a way that respects God's earth, and primarily space for God.

Too often our days are spent thinking about the future: we drive the kids to school or drive to work while planning what we shall do that day, on autopilot, hardly noticing anything or anybody we drive past. As we WhatsApp a friend, we are thinking about what we shall have for lunch, and fail to hear what she is really saying. We shove a plastic container in the microwave and eat its contents while thinking about a later meeting.

Simple living is about being joyfully *aware* of what we do, and why we do it. We can live in the present as well as the future, having the room to savour each moment of our lives. Above all, simple living is about getting rid of the clutter in our lives that gets in the way of our relationships with God, others, the wider natural world and ourselves, so that we can hear the voice of God more clearly and serve him more readily. As we do that, we shall discover what it really means to be rich, for simplicity is not about meanness and poverty, but about true abundance, about having life to the full. (See what Jesus said about fullness of life in John 10:10.)

Already, from what has been said so far, it will be apparent how this subject is relevant to the theme of this book. We might say that the concept of simplicity consolidates much of what we have looked at previously. Many people are recognizing there is something that needs changing in our lives. We live in an extraordinary time, with communication and technical advances developing rapidly, medical science achieving 'miracles' and consumer choice at its highest, and yet with global inequality at an extreme. In the light of this, we have to ask ourselves the question that Micah asked (Micah 6:8), 'What does the Lord require of me?' In our world today, what does it mean to 'act justly and to love mercy'? How do I 'walk humbly' with my God? A Christian approach to simplicity provides a helpful answer.

As we saw in 'N is for Needs', our culture today is consumer-based. It is profoundly self-centred and individualistic, placing value in the things we possess, and giving prestige to those who indulge themselves in luxury and waste and sell themselves as commodities for us to watch and follow. We have created a short-term, throwaway culture.

It is into this context that simplicity speaks. Simplicity leads us to turn our attention away from accumulating possessions, and instead encourages us to focus on our relationships – with God, others, the wider creation and ourselves.

There is much we could look at here, and I explore this in much more depth in *Just Living: Faith and Community in an Age of Consumerism*. But the area I want to look at here is our *time*. Time is God's creation and his gift to us. He has given it to us to enjoy and use for his service. We each have it in equal amounts, and how we choose to use that time is our responsibility. Simple living allows time to be the most rewarding and beautiful possession we have, helping us reach a place of wholeness and awareness.

And yet, 'I haven't got time' is a frequently heard complaint. As a result, many of us are suffering, with stress, sleep problems and relationship pressures becoming increasingly common. What is also clear is that the situation is only going to get worse. As writer, thinker and life-lover Tom Sine says, 'That means we shall have less time for family and friends, less time to pray and study Scripture and less time to volunteer to address the mounting needs of the poor in our societies.'[1]

One of the greatest ironies is that time often seems directly disproportional to the amount of money we have. Time is one of the greatest dividers: between those who spend time to save money and those who spend money to save time. As Roy McCloughry has said, 'The new materialism is to do with our attitude to time.' Time has now become a status symbol: we measure our worth by our busyness, and believe ourselves to be indispensable to all that goes on around us.

Our use of time reflects the values of our lives, and now is a good time to ask ourselves whether or not we are truly living out God's values. If not, what needs to change? I would encourage all of us to make changes so that we have the time simply to be: to be with ourselves and to be with God.

For many, a helpful way for this to happen is through the practices of silence, solitude and contemplation. Let us touch the surface by looking at the US psychiatrist and theologian Gerald May's three suggestions as to how we can begin to create space.[2]

First, he suggests looking for spaces that occur normally in our lives. Perhaps there are times that we automatically fill by scrolling through Facebook, Instagram or Twitter or making ourselves a drink, but that we could make 'intentional': moments to stop and be still. Ironically, there are apps that can help us do this, though I suggest trying to do without them if you can!

Second, we should try to find the more regular, set-aside spaces during the day that are 'simply and solely dedicated to just being'. However long, they are an opportunity to take some space and establish ourselves with Jesus at the centre. If you're able to, go outside: there is growing evidence that blue and green landscape elements are good for our health and well-being. After a long day of meetings in the Tearfund office, I go for a walk through the nearby park for forty-five minutes or so. It regulates my breathing (again, there is evidence that doing something rhythmic such as walking is good for stress), and allows me space to hand whatever has happened that day to God.

Finally, May recommends building longer spaces into our lives for authentic retreat. These may involve actually going away for a retreat or just taking a day of quiet.[3]

Our aim is to bring our use of time under control so that it serves our kingdom values rather than those of the world, living intentionally in each moment of time. Henri Nouwen's description of this is beautiful. He talks of a life

> in which time slowly loses its opaqueness and becomes transparent. This is often a very difficult and slow process, but full of re-creating power. To start seeing that the many events of our day, week or year are not in the way of our search for a full life, but the way to it, is a real experience of conversion. If we discover that writing letters . . . visiting people and cooking food are not a series of random events which prevent us from realizing our deepest self, but contain in themselves the transforming power we are looking for, then we are beginning to move from time lived as *chronos* to time lived as *kairos*.[4]

Time is a good place to start a consideration of simplicity, because it teaches us the importance of an inner simplicity, something we touched on in 'A is for Activists', where we saw the importance of prayer in our activity. As simplicity touches our approach towards money, the food we eat, the clothes we wear and so on, we remember that it begins with our heart attitude, and only then moves on to our outward practice.

This book is about inspiring you to 'act justly and to love mercy'. Simplicity has these things at its heart, and is desperately needed today. As Richard Foster says in his writings on simplicity, 'Our task is urgent and relevant. Our century thirsts for the authenticity of simplicity; the spirit of prayer, and the life of obedience. May we be the embodiment of that kind of authentic living.'[5]

**Action points**

- Foster has ten principles of simplicity:
    1. Buy things for their usefulness rather than their status. (But bear in mind too the lovely words from William Morris of the Arts and Crafts Movement at the end of the 1800s, to 'have nothing in your house that you do not know to be useful, or believe to be beautiful'. We don't need to live in a sterile environment; we just need to accumulate less stuff.)
    2. Reject anything that is producing an addiction in you (very relevant in our digitally addicted age!). Learn to distinguish between a real psychological need, such as cheerful surroundings, and an addiction.
    3. Develop the habit of giving things away.
    4. Refuse to be propagandized by the custodians of modern gadgetry.
    5. Learn to enjoy things without owning them.
    6. Develop a deeper appreciation for the natural world.
    7. Look with a healthy scepticism at all 'buy-now, pay-later' schemes.
    8. Obey Jesus' instructions about plain, honest speech. 'All you need to say is simply "Yes," or "No"; anything beyond this comes from the evil one' (Matthew 5:37).
    9. Reject anything that breeds the oppression of others.
    10. Shun anything that distracts you from seeking first the kingdom of God.
    Which of these strike you as interesting or particularly challenging for you? As you read them through, bear in mind the question from author Marie Kondo: 'Does this item spark joy?'

- Develop one practice that allows you to stop, and builds space for quiet in your life.

## Notes

1. Tom Sine, *Mustard Seed Versus McWorld: Reinventing Life and Faith for the Future* (Baker, 1999), p. 128.
2. Gerald May, 'Entering the Emptiness', in Michael Schut (ed.), *Simpler Living: Compassionate Life: A Christian Perspective* (Earth Ministry, 1999), pp. 50–51.
3. To look more closely at building space into our lives and practising silence, see the section on time in *Just Living: Faith and Community in an Age of Consumerism* (Hodder & Stoughton, 2016).
4. Henri J. M. Nouwen, 'Contemplation and Ministry', in Michael Schut (ed.), *Simpler Living*, p. 54.
5. Richard J. Foster, *Freedom of Simplicity: Finding Harmony in a Complex World* (HarperCollins, 2005), pp. 8–9, 14.

# T IS FOR TECHNOLOGY

If ever there was a word destined to produce both love and loathing, it has to be technology. The most wonderful thing and the solution to all our problems, or the devil's spawn leading to a dysfunctional society fixated with phones?

Me? I love technology. How could I say anything else when I'm using it at this very moment to write this book! I thank the Lord for technology every time I drive to a speaking engagement and arrive stress-free because I've been able to use my sat nav rather than struggle with holding a map in one hand and driving with the other, in the rush hour or in the dark.

I get the devil's spawn thing though too, of course. My personal email account is currently down, and I feel useless and disempowered as I work out what to do about it. While I'm sitting here writing, I'm aware of my work emails piling up, and I've turned off my phone so that doesn't distract me. And I've noticed a couple of DMs on Twitter– should I look at those quickly?

The word itself is very vague, and can mean anything from combustion engines to cloud-based apps. However vague though, we know that our societies and economies are completely dependent on a whole host of technologies which help us achieve a great many things – but they have widespread and often unseen impacts too. Technology undergirds every chapter in this book: society, as we know it, is enabled to happen because of technology.

Although technology has been slowly advancing throughout the history of humanity, the Industrial Revolution, powered by colonialism and the slave trade, was where technology came into its own. It literally changed the social and physical landscape of the UK, and from there to so many other parts of the world, laying the foundations for contemporary society. Thinkers such as John Ruskin and William Blake decried the resultant purge of the countryside, with 'dark Satanic mills' full of people subjugated to the processes of profit in the name of progress. 'Luddites' is a term we use today for people who are seen as standing in the way of progress, or struggling to know how to use their new phone – I remember when it referred to people who couldn't programme their video machine – but originally they were an early group of mill workers who destroyed new machinery because it threatened their jobs.

Fast-forward over 200 years and we find ourselves in a society with a dizzying array of technology, the scale of which is leading commentators to refer to this as the fourth 'digital' industrial revolution (the rise in electricity being the second, and the advent of computers the third). Ironically, some is now designed to help us do the things we did before we were so technologically subsumed: we have apps to help us exercise and walk more; one daughter has an app that encourages her to drink more water by rewarding her with cute little virtual plants each time she registers she has drunk something, and there is an app that tells her how many times she has interacted with her phone and had 'screen time', encouraging her to put the phone down and do something else. That surely is beyond irony.

Although technology lies behind probably every activity that we will do today, we will experience it most obviously in the televisions, computers, social media and smartphones that dominate our lives. This is one of the areas that has experienced the most change since I first wrote *L is for Lifestyle*. As I said in the Introduction, I don't think I even had a mobile phone back then, and my children can't believe that I handwrote all my university essays and didn't have a computer until well into my adult life. The digital revolution has transformed how we consume media, enabling us to stream films and music whenever we want. Complex algorithms shape our online purchasing decisions, and many of our core industrial processes would be unrecognizable to Ruskin and Blake as a result of artificial intelligence and robotics.

It is here that we encounter that ambiguity again (loving and loathing). These things have brought us so much that is good – I love our family WhatsApp groups that keep us in contact with one another, so different from when my dad used to travel and we wouldn't hear from him at all while he was away. Television has been an incredible educator – Tearfund started because people saw poverty and hunger for the first time in the 1960s and wanted to respond, and who can forget the amazing response to plastic pollution generated by millions of people in the UK watching *Blue Planet II* with David Attenborough? Computers and social media have enabled a new wave of social organizing, and been an integral part in revolutionary movements such as the Arab Spring in

2010/11 and the #MeToo campaign against sexual harassment and assault.

And yet, of course, they are also deeply problematic. There is a growing body of evidence showing that prolonged time spent with screens contributes to a decreased sense of well-being, complementing what we have seen in the previous chapter around the demonstrable benefits of getting outdoors. And I am interested in how social media has turned us into products as well as consumers: we might think we are consumers of social media, but actually we have *become* products, and advertisers are the real buyers, via algorithms analysing vast reams of personal data, so that specifically targeted information can be directed to the right consumers. I was taken aback to notice that shortly after looking online at an ethical shoe company I was researching for this book, the company now appears constantly in my FB feed and on Twitter. How much are we in control of the technology in our lives, or does it control us?

There is much more that could be said about the personal and cultural impacts of living in our technologically dominated society, but less well known are the environmental impacts. In fact, the manufacture, use and disposal of ICT equipment account for approximately 2% of global emissions – the same as aviation – and yet we talk lots about flying, but little about our technology usage. About a quarter of these emissions come from the impact of the data centres which house IT equipment, such as servers and data storage, and around half from their actual use, particularly in offices. The remaining quarter is accounted for by the manufacture and disposal of devices.

Another concern is the materials used to make devices (some of which are highly hazardous), and especially the need for 'rare earths': the seventeen chemical elements found in the Earth's crust whose unique elements make them essential for our high-tech products. Ninety per cent of rare earths mined come from China, and the environmental and health impacts are shocking. The Democratic Republic of Congo is also a country blessed by rich elemental deposits, but the story of the extraction of those deposits (cobalt being one of the key ones) is a tangled web of poverty, misery and environmental devastation.

There is good news though too, because technology also has the power to do a huge amount of good, even playing a part in reducing the impacts of its own usage. A friend of mine, Dr Richard Bull from Nottingham Trent University, has found that over 20% of out-of-hours energy consumption at his former university was due to IT equipment and lights being left on overnight and at weekends. Smart meters and controls are enabling the more efficient management and visualization of energy consumption in buildings. In the home, for example, smart meters and displays can encourage better behaviour by giving us real-time energy consumption levels: research has shown that we consume less when we actually understand more about our energy consumption. Human nature seems to need these motivators to help us change our behaviour.

But technology can go a lot further than this too, and there are so many ways in which technology is being used to bring about good. There are solar water pumps in areas suffering longer and more intense droughts; and apps that a) alert farmers when rains are coming and help them to know when to plant, and b) can help them to know the right market prices for their goods so they can ensure they get a fair price. There are renewable energy systems that can be used in refugee camps, improving the lives of some of the world's most vulnerable people, and early-warning systems to help communities prepare for floods. Digital technologies are enabling 'smart cities' to analyse and integrate electricity consumption, travel and water data in order to achieve greater efficiencies and align consumption patterns with renewable energy supplies. The rise in electric cars, autonomous vehicles and innovative car-sharing platforms have the potential to transform mobility, and this will increase efficiency and reduce carbon emissions. Both solid-state wave energy, which could better harness wave power, and carbon capture are technologies that may well be used more in future years. Maybe we will one day be driving on smart highways surfaced with solar tiles, and be housed in living buildings that grow food, produce waste in a way that nourishes the land, and are net-positive with their water and energy.

That sounds good to me!

**Action points**

- Become more mindful of technologies that are part of your everyday life. Ask yourself questions such as:
  1. Why was this made?
  2. Does it have a good impact on human work/ well-being?
  3. Is it a good solution to whatever problem it was trying to solve?
  4. Are there other solutions to this problem?
  5. Why is it still used? Why are other solutions not used?
- Build in regular times when you turn off all your screens and do something totally different, for example, go for a walk, talk to the other people in your house, cook, bake, knit, sew, garden, build, rest, read . . .

- If you work in an office, find ways to ensure all computers and lights are turned off at night. Laptops can use as little energy as a third of desktops, so could your work move to laptops as equipment needs replacing?
- Take a look at Practical Action's work, <https://practicalaction.org>, which focuses on using technology to help end poverty.
- Buy second-hand computers and phones (or make sure your next phone is a Fairphone), and make sure you recycle your ICT equipment.

# U IS FOR UNWANTED PEOPLES

Refugees have changed from being people on the other side of the world to people who look like us, wear the same clothes as us, and are trying to enter 'our' country for help, and often to be reunited with family members. In this chapter we are going to meet four people. Each one illustrates something of the situations faced by the world's most unwanted peoples: refugees.

Kalim came from a country ruled by a dictatorship. Ethnic conflicts and jealousies, provoked by the economic successes of the minority grouping, had led the majority group to use their political strength to gain dominance. Now the minority grouping was facing persecution and oppression. All the men were forced to do hard labour, and family members were routinely murdered. One day Kalim saw one of his people being publicly beaten. Enraged by the injustice, he killed the perpetrator. When the dictator learned of this, he tried to kill Kalim. Kalim knew his only option was to flee, and he became a refugee in a nearby country.

The refugee problem today is vast. The UNHCR defines a refugee as 'someone who has been forced to flee his or her country because of persecution, war or violence. A refugee has a well-founded fear of persecution, for reasons of race, religion, nationality, political opinion or membership in a particular social group.'[1] Their latest figures estimate that there are 25.4 million refugees around the world, more than half of whom are under eighteen years old. Syria is the largest country of origin, accounting for some 6.3 million refugees (a quarter of the refugee population), followed by Afghanistan (2.6 million refugees) and South Sudan (2.4 million refugees). Together with Myanmar and Somalia, these five countries account for over two-thirds of all refugees. Turkey hosts the largest overall population of refugees (3.5 million), followed by Pakistan, Uganda, Lebanon and Iraq. Overall, developing countries host 85% of the global refugee population (Europe hosts 10% and the Americas 3%). In addition, there are 3.1 million refugees who are 'asylum seekers', applying for permanent sanctuary, legal protection and material assistance in their host country, who must be able to demonstrate a well-founded case for persecution at home.

Incredibly, one in every 110 people globally is now an asylum seeker, refugee or IDP (Internally Displaced Person). Europe may not take in as many refugees as other parts of the world, but those of us living in Europe have been brought face to face with the crisis – sometimes literally, as tourists sun themselves on beaches where refugees are landing after terrible boat journeys. Many people die trying to cross the Mediterranean: the numbers change all the time, but most years see between 2,000 and 3,000 people lose their lives. There are many who want to reach the UK, but are living in northern France, in desperate conditions, just on the other side of the Channel.

War and ethnic conflicts are two of the main factors that cause people to become refugees. The war in Syria has seen an estimated 500,000 people die or go missing (the exact numbers are very hard to determine), devastated cities and the largest refugee crisis of our time. Over 1 million Rohingyan people have now fled Myanmar as a result of religious violence, walking hundreds of miles to Bangladesh. Most now live in squalid refugee camps, with high rates of malnutrition and a growing risk of cholera and other water-borne diseases.

Tamba and his family were facing starvation. Throughout the region the crops had failed and there was no food. In desperation, Tamba sent his sons to the neighbouring country where there was plenty of food. Through an amazing series of events, his sons met one of the members of the government, who personally gave them permission to bring over the whole family, and granted them a special permit to stay until the famine had ended.

Families comprise a large proportion of the refugee population. We saw earlier that over half (53%) of refugees are under the age of eighteen. Child refugees are extremely vulnerable, and the lack of income-earning opportunities forces many into exploitative livelihoods, such as joining fighting forces or prostitution. By contrast, Tamba's sons were exceptionally lucky.

Tamba and his family were forced to seek refuge elsewhere because of the wide-scale crop failure. Incredibly, more people become refugees through environmental disasters than for any other reason. The UNHCR states that there are 22.5 million displaced people due to climate change and weather-related disasters. Most of them are in sub-Saharan Africa, South Asia and Latin America, and the World Bank estimates that by 2050 there could be more than 140 million environmental refugees in these regions alone due to climate change.

As a high-ranking army officer and best friend of the prince, Amoru was able to enjoy all the luxuries of life. His situation fell apart, however, when his public popularity made him an enemy of the jealous king, who made three attempts on his life. Living in a country that gave him no access to the law, Amoru fled from the capital and became a fugitive in the surrounding hills.

Internally Displaced Persons leave their homes for the same reasons as refugees, but stay within their own country. There are currently 40 million IDPs, double the number in 1992, and they are a subject of huge concern for the international community. Because they are still under the laws of the state from which they are fleeing, they are especially vulnerable as they are not protected by international law or eligible to receive international aid. In a country in the throes of civil war, many of the basic services may have been destroyed; there may be no well-organized camps to receive IDPs, and fighting may make it difficult for aid organizations to provide relief. Seventeen million IDPs are children who have been forced to leave their homes because of armed conflict or violence. According to UNHCR figures, IDPs (including children) are displaced from their homes for an average of seventeen years. Many live in fear, and are forced to move over and over again.

Mandelena became a refugee a number of years ago with her family. During those years she lost both her husband and two sons. Eventually she decided to return to the rural area in her homeland, accompanied only by her daughter-in-law, who insisted on coming with her although she was from an ethnic grouping different from Mandelena's. On returning home, however, it was clear that the outlook was bleak.

Overwhelmed by poverty, Mandelena's daughter-in-law was forced to beg from the men in the fields. Alone, she was vulnerable to sexual abuse.

Voluntarily returning home is generally seen as the best solution for displaced people, and the majority of refugees do prefer to return home, if able to do so safely, though many can't. In 2017, 5 million IDPs and refugees went home. Conditions can be very hard, however, if basic infrastructures are still inadequate or ethnic tensions simmer underneath, and countries such as Syria are going to take decades to rebuild.

Mandelena's story has a positive ending: she and her mother-in-law were able to return home, and a relative still living in the area looked after them. The plight of the majority of women refugees, though, is not so good. Half of refugees are female, and women and children make up over half of the population in refugee camps. Here they often face worse hardships than the men, rarely having a say in how a camp is run, or where services such as water tanks or toilets are sited, and they are vulnerable to prostitution and human trafficking. Unaccompanied child refugees have reached a record high, with their number increasing fivefold since 2010. While under the care of the UNHCR, girls are less likely to receive an education than boys.

As the numbers of refugees increase, so countries are becoming less and less willing to accept them. When an emergency situation leads to a massive influx, local communities can find their resources and environment stripped. This happened in the Karagwe district of Tanzania during the Rwandan crisis, when the local people's farms were taken over by huts for the refugees and their trees were destroyed for firewood. It is the poorer countries that bear the brunt of the global refugee problem. The richer countries should recognize their responsibility to help.

Although the scale of the problem is peculiar to our time, refugees were known in the Bible. In fact, our four stories are all based on biblical characters – Moses, Jacob and his sons, David, and Naomi and Ruth – and the Bible could be called a story of refugees, from Abraham through to the exilic Israelites, through Jesus' early days in Egypt, and the early Christians scattered around the Roman Empire due to persecution. In 'A is for Activists' we saw how the laws of the nation of Israel make particular reference to caring for those who are vulnerable, and this includes people from other countries – 'aliens'. Moses' story is especially instructive, because it is through the events he led that the foundation for Israel's laws of compassion was laid. As Deuteronomy 10:18–19 shows, Israel is to love those who are aliens *because* they too were once, in Egypt. Because of God's great compassion for them, so they are to show compassion to others (see also Isaiah 58:7 and Ezekiel 22:7).

This compassion and welcome is being demonstrated by Reach Church Derby, in the UK Midlands, which has teamed up with a refugee charity to form Welcome Churches, with the vision of seeing every refugee in the country being welcomed by a church. They themselves now have more than 100 church members from refugee backgrounds, and are helping other churches respond similarly. One of the things they do is put together a 'welcome box' which a volunteer will take to someone who has newly arrived, to introduce themselves and welcome them to the area.

St Martin's Church in Maidstone is another example. When their vicarage became vacant, the church decided, with their local council, to house a Syrian refugee family. The family faced so many challenges – language, local customs, transportation and especially the weather! But the church, local schools and council worked hard to help them settle into their new life and become as independent as possible. Within a year the children were speaking English nearly fluently, and had become integrated into the education system. The relationship between the family and the surrounding community has been very good and the family has been able to settle in and become familiar with English ways.

And this takes us back to the early church. The Christian apologist Aristides gives this description:

> They walk in all humility and kindness, and falsehood is not found among them, and they love one another. They don't despise the widow and don't upset the orphan. He who has given liberally to him who has not. If they see a stranger, they bring him under their roof and rejoice over him, as it were their own brother: for they call themselves brethren, not after the flesh, but after the spirit and in God . . . And if there is among them a person who is poor and needy, and they have not an abundance of necessaries, they fast two or three days that they may supply the needy with their necessary food.[2]

What an encouragement for us to live similarly today!

### Action points

- Sign up to receive the newsletters of those involved in refugee issues: UNHCR or other overseas development organizations and charities that work with refugees in the UK and/or abroad (e.g. Tearfund, Oxfam, Christian Aid, CAFOD, Refugee Action, City of Sanctuary, Save the Children, Church Mission Society, Médecins Sans Frontières). Allow your increased awareness to lead to other actions, such as letter-writing and offering financial support.

- Contact your local authority and offer practical help and support for refugees living in your community. This can range from helping families improve their English or helping children with their homework to offering transport to the shops or to doctor's appointments.
- Get your church responding too. Have a look at the practical action advice given at <https://ctbi.org.uk/how-the-churches-are-responding-to-the-refugee-crisis>, <https://focusonrefugees.org/practical-action/page/2> and <www.welcomechurches.org>.
- Read *The Lightless Sky: My Journey to Safety as a Child Refugee* by Gulwali Passarlay (Atlantic Books, 2015): a brilliant memoir of an Afghan boy's experiences as a refugee.

## Notes

1. See <www.unrefugees.org/refugee-facts/what-is-a-refugee>.
2. *The Apology of Aristides: On Behalf of the Christians*, 15.7.

# V IS FOR VOLUNTEERING

Gina runs the Fairtrade stall at her local church. David helps with young people's holidays for the RSPB. Jenny is a local tree warden and keeps an eye on the trees in the local area, making sure they aren't cut down without very good reason. Angela volunteers for the Citizens Advice Bureau, and Mike helps out with the local boys' football team. Jo helps with her local food bank, and Ian has set up a FoodShare scheme. Diane helps refurbish old tools, which are sent to newly qualified artisans who need them in Africa, and Pete makes birdboxes from old pallets, which are then sold by a local charity.

There are many more examples I could give, all part of the 41% of the UK adult population that volunteers, putting in an average of 1.5 hours a week, contributing around £23 billion a year to the national economy. In the US, the figure is lower, with only 25% of adults volunteering, but that still contributes an estimated $184 billion to the US economy, and I have no doubt some of you reading this are a part of those stats.

Sadly, the UK figures actually represent a 15% decline in volunteering since 2005 (as measured in volunteer hours), which is especially pronounced in the 25–34 and 55+ age brackets. Is this linked with other discussions in this book around our deepening consumer culture that not only teaches us to focus on ourselves, but has also created financial and cultural pressures that leave little time for activities outside work and family? The good news, though, is that there has been a 28% growth in volunteering among 16–24-year-olds, possibly because they have more free time and want to enhance their CVs.

Throughout the course of this book we have looked at a great many actions that we can take to be promoting God's justice in our world. Giving our time is a fantastic way of making a difference to the people around us and to the planet on which we live. We could help in a children's club or a homeless shelter, run a Fairtrade stall at church, work in a charity shop, look for ways to befriend the lonely – such a big problem in our society – or help at a lunch club for elderly people. We could use our business skills to help a local charity, teach IT, decorate or garden for someone, help run an Alpha group, get involved in local environmental work, help run an arts centre, build, cook, clean . . . The opportunities are endless.

Volunteering is a great way of putting our natural or learnt skills to other uses. It gives us the scope to take the activities we enjoy and use them for the benefit of others. It is a chance to do something completely different from our paid work, and it is a wonderful opportunity to live out the love that God has placed in our hearts for other people and his world.

There are also residential volunteering opportunities. These enable you to try things for a week or two, or to dedicate a longer period to working with an organization, living away from home. You can spend time with a care organization, an environmental conservation group or a charity dedicated to animal welfare. There are also various Christian opportunities, such as L'Arche homes for people with disabilities, the Lee Abbey retreat centre or conservation work with A Rocha UK.

For something completely different and very rewarding, try volunteering overseas. The popular time to do this is between school and university, or university and paid work. I went to Malaysia for five months after my A levels and worked with a Christian care association. Our elder daughter Mali volunteered with A Rocha Ghana, working on a pangolin project. The huge range of possibilities, however, means that this needn't be restricted to gap years, and increasingly people are taking time out to do such a trip mid-career or in retirement. Tearfund runs a brilliant volunteering programme where you can do (for example) two weeks in Malawi, three months in Bangladesh or six months in Cambodia on your own, as a group from church or even as a family. We need to balance going overseas with thinking about reducing how often we fly. But I believe this is one instance where it is justifiable. Research done for Tearfund by the Barna Group has shown that 77% of Christians who are actively responding to poverty have seen poverty with their own eyes during travel outside their own country, demonstrating the long-term impact such volunteering can have on the volunteer, let alone the communities they go to.[1]

Anybody, anywhere, can be a volunteer. Whether you are young, a student, at home with small kids, disabled, retired or hard at work, there is something for which you can volunteer. Employer-supported volunteering is a good way to help those who are working to find the time to volunteer. This is often done through a company's Corporate Social Responsibility programme, where employees are encouraged to take one or two paid days a year to volunteer at a community project. I have benefited from this myself because a woman called Alicia used her volunteering days from Ernst & Young to do some of the initial research for this new edition of the book. If you're an employer, running a volunteering scheme can be very beneficial, especially in attracting millennials who enjoy making an impact through workplace volunteering. It can lead to better employee recruitment and retention, improved staff skills and confidence, with higher staff morale, and to better team building and a good public image.

But the benefits of volunteering are not only felt by employers who encourage their staff in that direction. Volunteering brings many benefits: the sheer enjoyment of the activity, the satisfaction of seeing results, meeting people, a sense of personal achievement, the chance to learn new skills or gain a qualification, and the opportunity to achieve a position in the community. In addition, research by Oxfam found that more than 80% of UK employers preferred to recruit candidates with volunteering on their CVs. Similarly, a study by Deloitte found that 82% of US employers prefer candidates with volunteer experience.

If the statistics are anything to go by, some of you will be volunteers already. If you're not, consider whether you might have some time, however limited, to give. This chapter is perhaps the most practical outworking of all that we have been looking at so far, and gives a genuine opportunity to make a real difference to a situation you feel passionate about.

**Action points**

- Use these questions to help yourself think through what you might like to do:

1. How much time do you have a week for taking up a new commitment? Is that time in the evenings, at weekends or in the daytime?
2. What do you like doing?
3. What skills do you have?
4. How much responsibility do you want to take on?
5. Are you more focused on local, national or international issues?
6. List three issues that you are interested in. Do you already belong to, or have links with, groups that are taking up these issues?
7. Where do you want to volunteer: from home, in your local area, overseas?
8. What things do you not like doing?
9. Would you be prepared to put some money aside, either to help a cause or to provide yourself with information? If so, how much?
10. What do other people think about your plans? How will these plans fit in with family life?

- Contact your local volunteer bureau to discuss with them what opportunities there are.
- Go online to find out about opportunities through websites such as Do-It.org, VolunteerMatch, Idealist.org, USA.gov or Vinspired.
- Look into volunteering with organizations such as A Rocha, Christians Against Poverty, Christian Aid, Mission Care, Tearfund, Timebank or VSO (Voluntary Service Overseas).
- If you prefer to volunteer from home, look into online opportunities (sometimes called micro-volunteering) through websites such as UN Volunteers, Skills for Change, Create the Good or GlobalGivingTime.

## Note

1. Barna Group and Tearfund, *Christians Who Make a Difference: The Unexpected Connections between Spiritual Growth and Caring for People in Poverty* (Barna Global, 2018).

# W IS FOR WATER

Many years ago I had a special holiday in Rajasthan, India. I was shocked when I got home to read that the area I'd been in was suffering from drought, and I thought back to the showers I had enjoyed each day and realized I had probably been taking that water away from others who needed it more than me.

Water is a powerful issue. Yet for most of us reading this, water is almost invisible. We use it throughout the day and hardly notice it as we flush the toilet, wash our hands, have a shower, fill the kettle . . . Water is, literally, on tap, and it is almost impossible to grasp what it must be like not to have easy access to clean water.

Currently 60% of the world's population (4.5 billion people) live in areas of water stress, where available water supplies cannot sustainably meet demand. Living in high water-stress areas, where the consequences of water shortages are more acute, naturally leads to problems with local food production and economic development. With global demand for water expected to grow by up to 50% by 2050, the situation looks set to worsen, and it is thought that, by then, 1.8 billion more people will live in water-stressed areas, of whom 80% will be in developing countries. The huge increase in global water demand, which is largely being driven by population growth, rising consumption, urbanization and energy needs, is increasing at substantially more than the rate of population growth. The biggest share of the world's water goes to agriculture, which consumes 69%, while industry consumes 19%, and the remaining 12% is used by municipalities for domestic purposes. Agricultural irrigation systems are often inefficient and waste huge amounts of water. In some developing countries, around 40% of irrigation water is lost to evaporation and run-off, never reaching the crops.

On top of increasing global demand, climate change is now a major contributor to water stress (where there is too little water) and water pollution (where there is too much, causing increased run-off and sewer overflow), as well as erosion and habitat damage. Climate change is resulting in more rainfall, and variability leading to more droughts and flooding, and food insecurity is set to increase where there is reduced rainfall. According to the World Bank, South African countries such as Botswana, Mozambique, Madagascar and Zimbabwe are particularly at risk.

As with so many environmental issues, it is the poor who suffer most, but are least responsible for the problems. As competition for water increases, the rich and powerful are the ones who will win. One major cause of water shortages is the migration of people to the cities, leading to a demand that far outstrips supply, as people desperately try to survive in slums and shanty towns. As the economic demands placed on poorer countries by rich nations include the privatization of public amenities, so water prices are hiked up in the cities. Water problems are becoming more severe too because of the increasing consumption of water due to economic development and growing standards of living. The tourism industry can make shortages worse, with hotels and golf courses taking water away from the local community.

The health implications of insufficient clean water are catastrophic, while armed conflict over dwindling water resources, particularly in the Middle East and Africa, will become an increasing threat. Years of drought in Syria, which caused widespread crop failure, is thought to have been one of the issues that led to the devastating war, and water scarcity is also thought to have been a contributing factor in recent conflicts in Libya, Yemen and Nigeria.

In the UK we are fortunate not to suffer from extreme water shortages to the extent that other countries do. Water is not, however, the limitless resource that we often think it is. The average person in the UK uses 980 litres of water a week, and the result is that the natural water-tables are lowering. Taking into consideration the extra problems that population growth and climate change will cause, the Environment Agency predicts that by 2050 there will be a significant deficit in water supply, particularly in the south-east of England, if we do not increase our water supply, reduce demand and cut down on wastage.

As well as having a devastating impact on the lives of people around the world, the shortage of fresh water is also severely affecting the ecosystems that rely on it. In the UK, for example, over-extraction is threatening rivers in many regions, leaving water levels too low to sustain their wildlife populations. English figures from the Joint Nature Conservation Committee show that only 32% of rivers that are designated as Sites of Special Scientific Interest (SSSIs) are classified as being in a favourable condition, and only 49% of freshwater habitats in standing water (though that is improving), leading to a very worrying decline in the wildlife that these places support.

Around the world the building of large dams to provide electricity can have major environmental impacts, including a decline in water accessibility and quality. There are currently 57,000 large dams on the world's rivers. A dam causes huge problems to the hydrological cycle of a river, and hence to its ecosystem, disrupting fish migration and leading to a decline in fish diversity and species. Alongside dams are the problems associated with providing water for irrigation. Perhaps the best-known example is the Aral Sea in the former Soviet Union, which has shrunk to a fraction of its original size due to the diversion of two inflowing rivers in order to provide irrigation water for cotton. This has devastated the area, ruining the former thriving fishing and tourism industry, and negatively changing the local climate.

Alongside the issue of water shortage is the extremely pressing problem of pollution and water sanitation. Thirty per cent of the world's population doesn't have access to safe drinking water. The result is that water-borne diseases from faecal pollution are a major cause of illness in developing countries. There is good news here, and deaths due to water pollution have been falling thanks to global efforts to improve water, sanitation and hygiene focused around Sustainable Development Goal 6, the target for water on sanitation agreed by the UN in 2015. Still, polluted water is thought to affect the health of at least 2 billion people, and to contribute to the deaths of around 800,000 children under the age of five annually.

In more industrialized countries a new range of pollutants keeps rivers and underground water supplies contaminated.

One of the biggest causes of pollution is intensive agriculture. The large amount of chemicals used results in some of it leaking into groundwater and rivers. Poisonous to wildlife, these chemicals can build up in plants and animals, with the result that they accumulate high levels of pesticides in their bodies. An increasing problem in industrialized nations is the paving over of natural areas to make paths, driveways and roads. When it rains, the water is not slowly soaked into the ground, but channelled into gutters and storm drains, which contain pollutants from dumped waste. The NRDC says that pollution from diffuse sources such as stormwater run-off exacerbated by paving is the biggest source of water pollution in the US.

As with so many of the issues we have looked at in this book, the problems here are huge and often beyond our control. Yet there are always things we can do to ensure that we are playing our part positively.

On a global level, we come back to 'L is for Letters', and our role in supporting the work of organizations by campaigning. This may mean writing to the big water companies, asking them to act responsibly when water is privatized in poorer nations. It might mean writing to our own government, urging them to meet SDG6, or to other companies that use a lot of water in making their products (e.g. drinks companies and cotton clothing manufacturers), asking them to reduce the water footprint of their products. Pepsi and M&S are already doing this, which is good news, but there is much more to be done, and we could urge a company to join the Water Footprint Network to help them do this.

At a local level there are steps we can all take to reduce the amount of water we use. We use the most water by showers (25%) and in flushing our toilets (22%), so finding ways to reduce our usage in these areas will have a major effect, such as having shorter showers and using a Hippo bag in our cistern. And I'm sure most of us have heard the saying, 'If it's yellow let it mellow; if it's brown flush it down!' After showers and toilets, the greatest amount of water is used in taking a bath or using hot water for personal washing (16%), then by washing machines (9%) and then in washing up (5%), with other cold water uses (such as washing the car or watering the garden) accounting for the remainder. With this in mind, we should make sure we take showers instead of baths, turn the tap off while brushing our teeth, and use our washing machines or dishwashers only when full (or wash up by hand). Water butts, of course, are a great way of saving rainwater for use on the garden. We can also use 'grey' water, in which we've washed ourselves, our dishes or our vegetables.

Underlying all of this is the recognition that our biggest water footprint actually lies in the things we consume – our 'virtual water'. For example, according to waterfootprint.org, the water footprint of a 150 g soy burger produced in the Netherlands is about 160 litres. A beef burger from the same country costs on average about 1,000 litres. Incredibly, a pair of cotton jeans uses 9,500 litres. Sadly for me, a 100 g chocolate bar costs 1,700 litres. And foods such as avocadoes, mangos and almonds all have a high water footprint. So what we have already seen in 'R is for Recycling' is vitally important here too: Consume Fewer Things.

Access to clean water is the most basic need we have, and water is fundamental to our living. No wonder the final picture in Revelation, the last book in the Bible, is of 'the river of the water of life, as clear as crystal, flowing from the throne of God and of the Lamb' (Revelation 22:1)! All of us need to do what we can to ensure that every person in our world has access, not only to the heavenly water but also to the earthly 'water of life'.

## Action points

- Write at least one letter or email to a company or an MP, asking that they take action on water.
- Support WaterAid, Practical Action, Charity:Water, Living Water International, UNICEF and other organizations working to improve water supply and quality for the world's poorest people.
- Make a note every time you use water today. Think through what you could do to use less.
- Become aware of your 'virtual water' usage. See <www.waterfootprint.org>.

# X IS FOR XENOPHOBIA

Ethnicity is perhaps the most politically charged issue of our day. We began to encounter it when we looked at the refugee crisis in 'U is for Unwanted Peoples', but we need to look it full in the face in this chapter. Xenophobia is defined in the Oxford Dictionary as 'Dislike of, or prejudice against, people from other countries', and I extend that out to a fear and hatred of those who are different, whether coming from another country, or born in the same one as ourselves. Brexit, terrorism and Islamophobia have all been a part of this. It simmers away under the surface of our cultures and erupted when Boris Johnson compared women in burqas to 'letter boxes', or when a black postgraduate student taking a nap in a Yale common room was woken by the police asking her why she was there. It erupted when an Iraqi and a Syrian man stabbed a German man to death, and when President Trump said that both sides were wrong after the white supremacist riots in Charlottesville. We see it in the Windrush scandal

where many people were held in limbo, despite the government apologizing for the deportations, and in the resurgence
of the Black Lives Matter campaign.

Xenophobia happens all round the globe. It is the cause of
the terrible atrocities we witnessed during the twentieth
century and have seen in this one. Racism happens at a global
level because, as David Haslam says, with its colonial roots,
'the poverty line is the colour line, everywhere. Black [or
brown, or yellow] almost always means poor . . . white means
wealthy.'[1] This fact has been evident throughout the book; so
many of the issues that we have been considering, such as
refugees or water, predominantly affect people who are not
white. Those of us reading this who are white may feel pretty
confident that we aren't racist. But one of the challenges of
this book is to consider where we may yet be contributing to
global racism, and how we can begin to change that, and one
of the challenges of this chapter is to recognize an implicit
bias that we all have, whatever ethnic background we may
come from.

The main focus of this chapter, though, is on racism at a
domestic, national level. Focusing on the UK, we are becoming
increasingly multi-ethnic, with 14% of the population of
England and Wales coming from ethnic minorities. Nearly
half (48%) live in London, where they comprise 40% of
residents. In Newham, the most culturally diverse borough,
the council reckons that over a hundred languages are spoken,
and it has the weakest standards of English, with 9% of
residents (25,000) unable to speak it. Poland was the most
common non-UK country of birth in 2017 – an estimated
1 million Polish nationals lived in the UK in 2017, and Romania
followed closely behind.

One important issue is employment and income. People in
minority ethnic groups are twice as likely to be unemployed

as people of white British descent, and Bangladeshi people have the highest rate (11%). In 2016 it was found that among 16–24-year-olds, 12% of white people were unemployed, compared with 23% of people in other ethnic groups. Not surprisingly, therefore, Pakistani and Bangladeshi households are more reliant on social security benefits and tax credits, which make up 25% of their gross income. Overall, people from minority ethnic groups are more likely than people of British descent to live in low-income households. Indeed, almost 30% of Pakistani and Bangladeshi people live in the most income-deprived 10% of neighbourhoods (though that has been improving, as fifteen years ago the figure was 60% of Pakistani and Bangladeshi people).

People from mixed, black and Asian groups are most at risk of becoming a victim of crime, and hate crimes (78% of which are racially motivated) are rising steeply, and they do so especially after a terrorist attack. Online hate crime too is increasing, despite being made illegal across the EU in 2008. And there is the ongoing increased suspicion of being a perpetrator of crime too – in France, young men of Arab and African descent are twenty times more likely to be stopped and searched than any other male group. (It is interesting to note that in France, attitudes towards black and Muslim populations are becoming increasingly hostile, even though their 2018 World Cup team was majority black, with some Muslim members.)

In the midst of the massive social problems that exist around race, we mustn't miss the positive, such as the coverage of the 2018 Royal Wedding which welcomed Meghan Markle's mixed-race background, and was regarded as a celebration of black culture. As I write this, we are in the middle of Black History Month, and yesterday Bishop Wayne Malcolm spoke powerfully at our Tearfund staff prayers, looking at the place of Africa in the story of the Bible (e.g. Ethiopia was known by the Hebrews as Cush, and is mentioned in Genesis 2:13 as being one of the lands that had the 'four headwaters' from Eden flowing through it, and if you bear in mind that Egypt is in Africa, and replace Egypt with Africa each time, it makes a startling difference).

But we have to recognize that we live in a deeply divided nation – and one in which so many people aren't even aware of the divides because they rarely encounter them in their own lives.

Although we looked at the issue of refugees at a global level earlier, we cannot discuss racism in the UK (or in the US, or whichever country you are from) without considering the issue of immigration, which is now one of the most politically polarizing issues in Europe and the US. Readers of this book will have different views regarding asylum policies. Countries and nationalities are important in giving people a sense of security and identity. If immigration controls are too open and the labour market becomes flooded, the finite resources of the welfare and education system will break down, unable to cope with the numbers. Nevertheless, the fact is that the UK does not receive as many asylum seekers as some parts of the media claim. Including asylum dependants, the UK had the sixth highest number (39,000) of asylum applications within the EU in 2016. The UK asylum system has become increasingly tougher over recent years, in response to the refugee crisis that we saw in 'U is for Unwanted Peoples', and has inherent problems, leading to many asylum seekers being refused application, with no enquiry into whether they might be facing persecution or death when returned home. More positively, many asylum seekers have much to contribute to the UK, both financially and culturally. An HMRC report estimated that, between 2010 and 2014, EEA migrants in the

UK contributed £2.54 billion (though this does not include costs incurred by housing benefit and use of public services).

Despite this, racism demonstrated towards asylum seekers and refugees can make their lives a misery. Many asylum seekers arrive in a state of shock or trauma following horrific experiences, yet do not find support on entering the UK. Every year around 2,000 female asylum seekers are detained in the UK. A report submitted to the Home Affairs Committee by women's refugee organizations stated that among their sample of women refused asylum in the UK and not removed, 67% became destitute, 25% had been detained, 97% were depressed and 63% said they had contemplated suicide.

In 'A is for Activists' and elsewhere, we have noted the foundational principle that all people have been made in the image of God. One nation, Israel, was explicitly chosen to be 'his people' in order that all nations might be redeemed (Isaiah 49:6). God is manifestly the God and Creator of all people, and the Old Testament is not frightened to show God moving beyond the boundaries of his chosen people (e.g. in the stories of Ruth and Jonah and in the description of Cyrus, king of Persia, as his 'anointed' in Isaiah 45:1).

Our supreme model is Jesus, who refused to let racial boundaries stand in the way of God's love (e.g. Matthew 8:5–13; 15:21–28; Luke 9:51–55 and the parable of the Good Samaritan in Luke 10). Writing on 'loving the stranger', the Revd Dr Inderjit Bhogal says, 'Jesus has left an example for his community. Practise hospitality. Eat with one another. Eat with the most vulnerable ones. Eat with "the stranger". Our lifestyle should be one of hospitality and solidarity, not hostility and segregation.'[2] As Abraham showed hospitality to the three strangers in Genesis 18, so we too should be ready to open our doors to those who are not like us. The Emeritus Chief Rabbi, Dr Jonathan Sacks, quotes the Jewish sages who said, 'On only one occasion does the Hebrew Bible command us to love our neighbour, but in thirty-seven places commands us to love the stranger', and, he adds, 'The stranger is one we are taught to love precisely because he is not like ourselves.'[3] This is hard, and often we fear getting to know people who are different. Yet we need to have the courage to step across the divide and reach beyond ourselves.

As people following Jesus, racism cannot be something we tolerate. We must all take steps to see it eradicated.

### Action points

- Increase your awareness of ethnic minority issues. Keep a lookout for relevant television and radio programmes, read the *Asia Times* and *The Voice* (both available online), and check out podcasts by people such as Reni Eddo-Lodge.
- If 'V is for Volunteering' whetted your appetite, you could consider volunteering for a local asylum seekers' project or visiting an immigration detainee. (To find out more, see <www.aviddetention.org.uk>.)
- How aware of race issues is your church? Racial Justice Sunday is an initiative in the UK. Find out more and see if your church could take part.

### Notes

1. David Haslam, *Race for the Millennium: Challenge to Church and Society* (Church House Publishing, 1996), p. 210.
2. See <www.inderjitbhogal.com/category/sermons>.
3. Jonathan Sacks, *Faith in the Future* (Darton, Longman & Todd, 1995), p. 78.

# Y IS FOR YOUNG PEOPLE

When I was little, my mum looked out of her front window one winter's day to see two young girls standing out in the snow. When they were still there some time later, Mum went out and talked to them, and discovered that their mum had shoved them outside first thing in the morning and told them not to come back till evening. Mum invited them inside, and that was the start of a friendship with them that lasted all the way through their teens. Now grown up and with families of their own, they still pop in from time to time to say hello, and one of them has her own faith in Christ that goes back to those early years. They have had a rough life, but I wonder what else might have happened to them had they not had my mum to be a steady influence as they grew up.

One of the primary reasons for setting up the Community Association that I co-chaired for many years was to help the young people on our estate. There were growing problems from a specific group of young people: drug and alcohol abuse, physical and verbal violence against residents, petty crime and general anti-social behaviour. The problems on the estate were nothing new and had all the classic symptoms, with a high rate of teenage pregnancy, broken families, low education and few prospects, and just plain boredom.

The Community Association worked hard to see things change. I chaired a Community Action Partnership with the police, local council, youth service and housing association, which ensured that those agencies saw the estate as a priority, and coordinated their efforts to combat anti-social behaviour. We had youth representatives on the Community Association and, as a result, had a five-a-side and basketball area built on the green in the middle of the estate, and a youth shelter built next to it to provide a place where young people could hang out, away from the 'hot spots'. We have now had two community wardens for a long time, who work on the estate, listening, among other things, to what the young people say are their needs. They set up a Junior Community Warden scheme that works with particular youngsters, encouraging them to participate in estate life and take some responsibility for their area, and two volunteers from the Community Association run a gardening project that takes young people out on to the green, planting and making the place look nicer. We have had a 'Football in the Community' scheme each summer, run by players from Brighton and Hove Albion, which not only teaches football but also focuses on other lifestyle issues, such as health, discipline and respect for others.

We didn't expect to work miracles overnight, but we have shown the young people that they are worth listening to, and spending time and money on. In fact, it was a real privilege to see the estate change over the twelve years that the Community Association was in existence.[1] The community wardens have commented that they now come on to the estate to have a rest, and the social landlord has cut their estate walk-rounds from monthly to every other month because we 'have turned from being a bad estate into a good estate'.

Of course, the issues on my estate are nothing new, and are mirrored around the country. In fact, overall, a picture is building of a significant minority of young people throughout Europe and North America facing increasing pressures from contemporary society and struggling to cope. According to an NSPCC report, nearly 14% of 16–24-year-olds reported experiencing abuse during childhood, and in a US survey, 73% of students reported that they had been bullied at school. The NHS reports that one in ten children in the UK has mental health struggles, and eating disorders among people under twenty-five are growing alarmingly. The Children's Society 'Good Childhood Report' found that one in four fourteen-year-old girls has self-harmed.

In the fifteen years since this book was first written I have brought up two girls, and have seen the culture change and witnessed them (and their parents!) trying to cope with it. We have already touched on this, of course, in 'T is for Technology', but the biggest change has been the onslaught of screens. When my eldest was little, it was still appropriate to have 'no telly time', but that soon became inadequate, and we had to have 'no screen time' instead. The rise of screens and social media has led to issues such as cyber-bullying, and a new form of image pressure as social media feeds full of friends and celebrities posting photoshopped pictures of themselves give a distorted understanding of what 'normal' looks like. According to the Children's Society, in the UK 61% of young people had a first social media account at age twelve or under, and 46% of girls state that social media has had a negative impact on their self-esteem. As we have seen already in 'N is for Needs', there is big branding pressure from 'influencers' on social media sites – a multi-billion-dollar industry. Influencers are paid by brands to use their social media following as a platform from which to advertise products, by tagging them in posts. Instagram feeds become littered with ads, sometimes in a very subtle way, and this normalizes a constant need to buy new things. Not so subtle is when a celebrity does a 'haul' (take a look at fashion and beauty vlogger Zoella on YouTube doing a Primark haul), but the millions of fans love it, and sales rise as a result.

Whatever the problems, however, there are actions that all of us can take. Most simply, we can be a friend. How many of us reading this book would cite a youth worker, church leader, neighbour or teacher as having played a large part in our development as a child and teenager? One of the most striking aspects of juvenile crime figures is the small percentage of young people who commit the highest number of crimes. What a difference could be made if these young people were able to form relationships with those who would help them through life, as with my mum at the start of this chapter?

On a global level the current generation of young people is the largest in the history of the world – what is being called 'peak youth'. According to the UN, today's youth population is the largest in history: half of the world's population is younger than thirty (and a quarter under fifteen). There are significant things to be hugely thankful for. Child mortality rates have nearly halved since the last edition of this book in 2008. Eighty-eight per cent of one-year-olds now receive at least one vaccination. Ninety-one per cent of primary-school-aged children are now in school, and the number of children out of school worldwide has halved since 2000, thanks to the work being done around

SDG4 on quality education. Despite the challenges we have seen already, it is good news that young people around the world are at the forefront of the digital revolution, with 70% now online, thereby increasing their access to economic opportunities and social activism. And yet, when one considers that nearly nine out of ten young people live in the developing world, and that 500 million children and adolescents grow up in families surviving on incomes of less than £1.50 ($2) a day, it becomes clear that the problems faced by young people are immense.

AIDS is still the leading cause of death among young people (aged 10–24) in Africa, and the second leading cause globally – and young people are the only population group in which AIDS-related deaths are rising. Over the past thirty years or so of the epidemic, around 17 million children have lost one or both parents due to AIDS.

Despite the big gains in education, there are still 120 million primary-school-aged children out of school (around half of them girls). In Somalia only 23% of children attend primary school (though that is up from 12% twenty years ago). It hardly needs to be said how important good education is, both to individuals – developing qualities and giving them skills that can help them avoid dangers such as bonded labour or armed recruitment – and to the development of a country, which can be transformed in a single generation when education is improved.

Following on from education, employment is still also a big issue. According to the latest UN World Youth Report, unemployment affects more than 73 million young people worldwide, and in some countries the youth unemployment rate is now above 50%.

Many young people live in extremely vulnerable positions, facing armed conflict, bonded labour, a life on the streets and work in the sex industry, which continues to cause untold damage to millions of lives. And the kidnapping of school-girls by Boko Haram in Nigeria reminds us that crucial to the health, education and employment of young people is the status of women in a society. It is no coincidence that a map showing women's literacy rates reveals that nearly all the countries with under 30% are in Africa. In the Niger, a shocking 91% of women are illiterate. Where women are valued, girls are valued, and where girls are valued, the lives of all young people are improved.

The good news is that wherever in the world there are young people in trouble, there are people working to bring about change – and often that is through the young people them-selves. In the UK, for example, JustLove is a student group now in twenty universities, inspiring Christian students to act for justice, both locally and abroad. Their latest report shows they gave over 5,500 volunteer hours in local communities and raised nearly £13,000 for other charities. I've had the pleasure recently of meeting the Green Anglican young people of southern Africa and something called the Jos Green Centre in Nigeria – both groups that Tearfund supports – doing inspiring work to get the church in Africa active environmentally, and generating employment for young people around renewable energy and recycling. (I regularly wear a gorgeous bracelet made by the Jos Green Centre team from a plastic bottle and the scraps from a local tailor shop.) Malala Yousafzai has brought worldwide attention to the issue of the education of girls, and her organization still works to raise awareness of child marriage, war and discrimination, and also spotlights inspirational young women. And, while I've been writing this book, another inspiring example has been Greta Thunberg, who started a global series of strikes by schoolchildren to highlight the urgency of tackling climate change.

Let us bring positive change, both locally and globally, in our world.

### Action points

- Think about the young people in your neighbourhood or church. Are their needs and potential being met? Is there anything you can do, even if it's just being a friendly face? Perhaps 'V is for Volunteering' has already inspired you to do something! To get more involved, you could look at the mentoring opportunities offered by organizations such as XLP.
- Seek out opportunities to ask the children in your life about their internet usage and the things they read and watch. Encourage them towards a healthy relationship with technology and more face-to-face interaction.
- Look at the brilliant work being done by The Girl Effect, <www.girleffect.org>, and get your church youth group involved with #WeAreTearfund or The Christian Aid Collective.

### Note

1. For more on the story of what happened to the Whyke Estate Community Association, you will have to read *Just Living*!

# Z IS FOR ZEITGEIST

On a CD cover I read this:

> 'What is *Zeitgeist*?' we are continually quizzed. 'Spirit
> of the time', we nod, trying to look the part. 'Era defining',
> we occasionally add as a bit of a try on. We'll tell you what
> it is . . . It's trying to make some sense of this glorious mess.[1]

As I read that, it struck me that this is what we've been doing through this book: 'trying to make some sense of this glorious mess' – this glorious mess that is our world.

There is no doubt that we live in a beautiful world. Just consider the amazing beauty of the rainforests or the coral reefs; the skylark spiralling above the fields, the prairie dog scurrying along the ground or the water vole swimming through the rivers; the hibiscus and bougainvillea growing along the wall. As humans too, we have been richly blessed with the ability to form friendships and nurture our families;

with the means to travel and trade throughout the world, creating wealth and prosperity; with opportunities to develop our talents and potential, to build community and nourish our inner beings.

This most certainly is glorious. As we see continually, these blessings come from God who loves giving us good things. As we use them well, so the glory goes back to him.

But we also live in a mess. The spirit of the age blinds us to the origin of these good things, turns us away from our relationships and into ourselves, and causes us to see these gifts as being our own, to be used for our own ends. As with the good, so with the evil. It runs through every chapter of this book: greed and exploitation, selfishness and idolatry.

As people who don't want to conform to the spirit of the age, but who want to be transformed by the renewing of our minds (Romans 12:2), we must look carefully at the blessings we have received and ensure we are using them to bless others. The danger is that we can become hypnotized by our cultural norms and blinded to the possibilities we have to see change occurring.

The good news is that there *is* an alternative. The gospel has the power to break that hypnotism and enable us to change our lives so they may reflect the goodness of God and his blessing for his creation. What we are talking about here is moving from the spirit of the age to the kingdom of God, pictures of which we have looked at a number of times. As we do this, we move from the values of this present age and towards the values of the kingdom: values of selflessness and peace, of inclusivity and love for the world.

The kingdom of God is made visible through our prayers; through the concentrations of our worship; through our practice of the disciplines and the cultivation of the Christian virtues. The kingdom is also made visible on this earth through our actions. Each time we send off a campaign email or meet our MP, each time we look up and smile at a neighbour, each time we buy a Fairtrade product or take the trouble to leave the car at home or decide not to fly on holiday, we are playing our part in seeing God's kingdom come, now and into the future.

This book is a call to change our lives in order to respond to the many challenges facing our world, as a part of our Christian discipleship. The changes facing us are many and varied: for some they are easily implemented, while for others they demand wholesale adjustments. Whether we decide to engage in regular campaigning, move our investments, switch our energy provider, give more of our money away, change our eating/shopping habits or revolutionize our working situation – whether these decisions we make take us a month to carry out or the rest of our lives – the gospel of Jesus fills us with hope and with confidence that these changes are worth making.

And as you come to the end of this book, you can take courage in the knowledge that thousands of others have read it too and are making changes – and getting their churches engaged as well. By doing this, we are building into God's promised future, when there will be no more sickness or suffering, tears or death, and when all God's creation will freely worship him.

### Note

1. *Zeitgeist: New Wave Club Culture* (Stress Recordings, 1997).

# GLOSSARY

| | |
|---|---|
| 350.org | An international environmental organization addressing climate change, with the goal of reducing atmospheric carbon dioxide to 350 ppm (parts per million) from the current level of 400 ppm |
| CAFOD | Catholic Agency for Overseas Development |
| COP 21 | Conference of Parties, with 'parties' meaning the countries that ratified the UN Framework Convention on Climate Change (UNFCCC) in 1992 at the Earth Summit in Rio de Janeiro |
| DFID | Department for International Development |
| DfT | Department for Transport |
| Eco Church | An A Rocha UK project. Online survey and resources to help you and your church care for creation, to love our global neighbours and follow God faithfully: <https://ecochurch.arocha.org.uk> |

| | |
|---|---|
| EEA | European Economic Area |
| EPA | Environmental Protection Agency |
| EU CAP | Common Agricultural Policy of the European Union |
| EV | Electric vehicle |
| EWG | The Church of England's Environmental Working Group |
| FB | Facebook |
| FSC | Forest Stewardship Council |
| FT | Fairtrade |
| GDP | Gross domestic product |
| HMRC | Her Majesty's Revenue and Customs |
| ICT | Information and communications technology |
| IDP | Internally Displaced Person |
| IEA | International Energy Agency |
| IMF | International Monetary Fund |
| MSC | Marine Stewardship Council |
| NPI | New Policy Institute |
| NRDC | National Resources Defense Council |
| NSPCC | National Society for the Prevention of Cruelty to Children |
| NWF | The American National Wildlife Federation |
| REACH | Regulation on Registration, Evaluation, Authorisation and Restriction of Chemicals |
| RSPB | Royal Society for the Protection of Birds |
| RSPO | Roundtable on Sustainable Palm Oil |
| SDGs | UN Sustainable Development Goals |
| Snopes | Online fact-checking website, <www.snopes.com> |
| SOFIA | State of the World's Fisheries and Aquaculture report |
| SRIs | Socially Responsible Investments |
| SSSI | Site of Special Scientific Interest |

| | |
|---|---|
| *The Story of Stuff* | A short animated documentary about the lifecycle of material goods |
| TPI | Transition Pathway Initiative (an investment tool used by asset fund managers to assess how well or not a company is moving towards a low carbon economy) |
| UKROFS | UK Register of Organic Food Standards |
| UNEP | United Nations Environment Programme |
| UNFCC | United Nations Framework Convention on Climate Change |
| UNHCR | United Nations High Commissioner for Refugees |
| UNICEF | United Nations International Children's Emergency Fund |
| WasteAid | A charity training communities in simple and affordable waste management and recycling skills |
| WRAP | An organization working towards practical solutions to improve resource efficiency |
| WTO | World Trade Organization |
| WWF | World Wildlife Fund |
| XLP | The eXceL Project, a charity that works to create positive futures for young people growing up on deprived inner-city estates |